What
The
Jesus

What a Friend They Had in Jesus

The Theological Visions of Nineteenth- and Twentieth-century Hymn Writers

Harry T. Cook

POLEBRIDGE PRESS
Salem, Oregon

Cover design by Kitty Black
Interior design by Robaire Ream

ISBN: 978-1-59815-129-9

In honor of
Hazel Dickson
Dorothy Peterson
Pearl Smith
and thousands of others like them who taught a generation of
American children to sing the hymns of that old-time religion

Contents

Abbreviations

1,2 Cor	1,2 Corinthians
1,2 Pet	1,2 Peter
1,2 Thess	1,2 Thessalonians
1,2 Tim	1,2 Timothy
Col	Colossians
Deut	Deuteronomy
Eph	Ephesians
Exod	Exodus
Gen	Genesis
GPet	Gospel of Peter
Heb	Hebrews
Isa	Isaiah
Jer	Jeremiah
Lev	Leviticus
Matt	Matthew
Phil	Philippians
Ps(s)	Psalm(s)
Rev	Revelation
Rom	Romans

Biblical verses are the author's own translation unless otherwise noted.

Preface

It took me years to appreciate my upbringing in the Sunday school of a small Methodist Church in the smallest of northern Michigan villages in the late 1940s and early 1950s. The substance of that experience came in handy, in fact, when I arrived as a student in a graduate school of theology in the 1960s and found myself—at an elementary level at least—several steps ahead of many of my classmates because I not only knew the names of the books of the Bible in their order but had memorized plenty of the texts in them and even knew something of their supposed provenance.

Besides the biblical knowledge, I had also unwittingly internalized the theology and piety of that unique group of English and American hymnists who through their hymn writing had made the Jesus of New Testament mythology into a real, live human being, approachable as mentor, best friend, and confidant. Intellectually I had left all that behind in the process of earning a liberal arts degree in the study of philosophy, history and literature, guided by professors into the habits of critical thinking and synthesis. However, the emotional ties formed by the hymns remained, and to this day I go around the house or whilst on my morning power walks whistling or singing them to the apparent annoyance of birds, who seem to think the airwaves are exclusively theirs at dawn's early light. My wife has long since heard "enough already" of such hymns.

The tunes to which many of those hymns are set can be characterized perhaps uncharitably as musically obvious and overly chromatic, yet they are etched in memory along with their content—and that is not the only thing. The theology apparent in them is really an inflated christology that, to an orthodox systematic theologian, would seem to be almost oddly Unitarian in nature. I hasten to say that theology as a discipline seems to me to be both so arbitrary and abstract that no one should be discounted for focusing on one expression of an imagined deity over another—Father, Son, *or* Holy Ghost.

For the most part, the better known hymns of the period covered in this book feature the personage known as "Jesus" and the part the various images of that character of religious myth played not only in the hymns themselves but in the formation of a peculiar theology in which "the Son," as he is called by orthodox Christians, plays the central and sometimes the only role of both the transcendent and imminent deity associated with Protestant Christianity.

Hymn texts composed from the mid-nineteenth and well into the early twentieth century have been submitted here to the same exegetical discipline as one would biblical texts. In each case efforts have been made to tell the story of the hymnist responsible for each text, the demographical setting in which the text was composed, and other details that will to some extent reveal what the writer may have been thinking, experiencing, and believing as his or her pen was set to paper.

The focus of the analysis will be the theological images and language of the texts, the human needs and emotions revealed in them and the culture they reflect with respect to gender roles, home life, education and events current at the time they were written.

The process of analyzing the hymn texts is intended to yield a concise and accessible history of Protestant piety in the America of the 1830s through the 1930s along with the relevant political, socio-economic demography that may have affected the composition of those texts.

Two questions will be posed, and answers to them are of a contingent nature offered to the thoughtful reader: 1) to what extent the theology produced by or represented in the hymn texts may have influenced the articulation of American evangelical theology, and 2) to what degree that theology has survived in evangelical churches of the twenty-first century.

It is important for me to establish at the outset that this work is by no means intended to belittle the hymns texts, their authors, or the beliefs of those authors or of those who have sung them down the years. The author of this book is as far from being an evangelical Christian as the tree visible outside his study window is from being the cat at his feet. Yet he honors that tradition and was once part of it, if only in the singing of those hymns that tell of that "old, old story." There is present in the hymnody treated of in this book a newer form of hymn text in which the social gospel, the issues of war and peace and even geopolitics are represented. These, too, were part of my religious experience, but in my teen and high school years.

I was able to write the substance of this book primarily on the strength of having been tutored in Greek New Testament and taught homiletics by George A. Buttrick, as well as theology and the history of its development by Paul B. Hessert—both, now, of blessed memory. I mention, too, the late David Lott Strickler, in whose choral music class I sat in my undergraduate years and in whose college choir I learned so very much about hymnody and the difference between hymns that matter and hymns that don't. Finally, and perhaps of even greater importance, I owe to those women to whom this book is dedicated my familiarity, annoying as it can sometimes be, with the hymns under consideration here. Most of the hymns do not fit in either words or music my adult approach to and appreciation of aesthetics, the philosophy of religion, or, for that matter, my perception of reality. Yet, entirely without my realizing it, those hymns became for better or worse the emotional bedrock on which my intellectual structure rests in matters of religion, its history, and literature.

Among those whose efforts on this book's behalf must be acknowledged are David Nisbet Stewart, a church musician of impeccable credentials as well as a composer of note, who read the manuscript and made helpful comments. Dr. Josephine A. Kelsey, a long time friend and mentor, contributed important suggestions. The likes of Larry Alexander of the Polebridge Press and Cassandra J. Farrin, who edits manuscripts for proper English usage, are indispensible to any author's attempts. They certainly have been to me. I am grateful to my eldest son, Dr. Robert C. Cook, assistant professor of music theory at the University of Iowa, for his most valuable advice concerning the musical mechanics of early chants and liturgical singing. The keen eye of my wife, Susan M. Chevalier, a professional editor, is always helpful when the galley proofs arrive. I am always reassured by her expertise and buoyed up by her never-failing love and support.

—Harry T. Cook

Part I
Context of Church and Culture

Introduction

A Brief History
of Hymnody

The English word *hymn* is lifted whole cloth from the Greek ὕμνος, meaning in New Testament Greek "a song of praise to gods or heroes"[1] and in Homeric Greek simply "strain, lilt or melody."[2] Thus, clearly out of this language tradition a "hymn" has always been of two parts: words and music. Whether or not the Epistle to the Colossians is entirely of Pauline provenance remains up for debate in the biblical scholarship community, but a hint to early Christian liturgical practice can be gleaned in Col 3:16: "Let the word of Christ dwell in you richly . . . and with gratitude in your hearts, sing psalms, hymns and spiritual songs to God" (NRSV). It is helpful to be able to note that the author of Colossians groups psalms (presumably those 150 in the Hebrew document known as *Psalms*) with those things that were sung by communities of primitive Christianity.

From primitive tribal chants to national anthems to college almae matres to the drinking songs of such spectacles as the Oktoberfest, people for time out of mind have sung together in acts of unity. It is not for nothing that most hymns are sung "in unison." Such singing can create bonds where there are none and strengthen those already in place, as in when young Germans, besot with beer, brayed the Horst Wessel song in the early euphoria of Nazi-dom. An auditorium full of Germans triumphant in the early victories of Adolf Hitler singing "*Deutschland, Deutschland über alles*" was an aural blitzkrieg. The St. Olaf College Choir singing *Ein feste burg ist unser Gott* [*A Mighty Fortress Is Our God*] could make a Lutheran, at least temporarily, out of the most brittle of Unitarians. And for a genuine spine-tingling thrill, listen to the crowd on the last night of the Proms in Britain belt out Thomas Arne's "Rule, Brittania."

Hymns, then, are vehicles of evangelization and catechesis as well as a means of bonding. It is unclear exactly to what Col 3:16 refers in terms of "hymns," but examples of what may have been early hymns include Phil 2:5–11 (NRSV):

> Christ Jesus, though he was in the form of God
> did not regard equality with God
> as something to be exploited
> but emptied himself, taking the form of a slave being born in
>   human likeness
> and being found in human form,
> he humbled himself and became obedient to the point of
>   death—even death on a cross.
> Therefore God has highly exalted him and gave him the name
>   that is above every name
> so that at the name of Jesus every knee should bend, in
>   heaven and on earth and under the earth,
> and every tongue should confess that Jesus Christ is Lord, to
>   the glory of God the Father.

The author's research—and that of many others—suggests that parts of the prologue to the Gospel of John (1:1–18) may have been in their inception strophes of a hymn or hymns to the incarnation.

It is obvious that texts set to singable and memorable tunes tend to be remembered more readily than texts by themselves. When I attempt to recite the text to the alma mater of my college, I falter. When I sing it to the bass line of the four-part harmony of the tune, as I did numerous times as a member of the college choir fifty-odd years ago and since then at alumni events, it comes out correctly.

Ignatius of Antioch was wont to employ musical metaphors, and in one in his seven famous letters—this one to the Ephesian church, he wrote: "Your presbytery (college of bishops), indeed, which deserves its name and is a credit to God, is as closed tied to the bishop as the strings to a harp. Wherefore your accord and harmonious love is a hymn to Jesus Christ."[3]

Yet whatever Ignatius would have heard by way of chants and hymns would have been sung to whatever melodies local churches would have learned. Until the ninth century, tunes varied from place to place and over time. Indeed, until the late eleventh century liturgical singing—chants and hymns—were performed from rote memory. What notation existed was imprecise, *aide-mémoires* for singers already familiar with the repertoire. It was repetition that fixed—or didn't fix—the music of the chants. Not much, if any, uniformity seemed to have existed until a choral director named Guido of Arezzo—Arezzo being a city in Italy about fifty miles southeast of Florence—laid before Pope John XIX the musical staff and what we know today as the *ut (do), re, mi, fa, sol, la* method of learning and remembering melodies. Meant originally as tools for teaching forgetful young singers, these two innovations helped make it possible systematically to record and preserve the as-yet undivided Catholic Church's liturgical chants. Guido's genius helped make possible later polyphonic music as most churchgoers in modern times would know it.

The monks of the Middle Ages set Latin texts to plainsong which later were re-set to polyphonic scores and later yet to metric settings complete with four-part harmony. In the Church of England metrical psalms, such as the well-known hymns based on the 23rd Psalm—"The Lord's my shepherd, I'll not want," from the Scottish Psalter of 1650; *My Shepherd Will Supply My Need*, by Isaac Watts; and *The King of Love My Shepherd Is*, by Henry Williams Baker—became for a time the steady diet of congregational music. It was left to Isaac Watts (1674–1748) basically to invent modern congregational singing of hymns. Watts was born into a nonconformist family and grew up in dissenter Protestantism. He showed proficiency at an early age with the construction of rhymed verse. Not permitted to attend Cambridge or Oxford due to his nonconformist background, he studied Hebrew, Latin, and Greek at Stoke Newington academy and later became the minister of a London chapel. Watts broke from the hidebound tradition of John Calvin, who strictly limited hymn texts to translations and occasional paraphrasing of psalm texts. Watts converted such texts into metrical versions, making them easier for non-musicians to sing. He also introduced extra-biblical phraseology into newer texts, as he does in *When I Survey the Wondrous Cross* and *How Wondrous Great, How Glorious Bright.*

In *The Hymnal 1982* of the Episcopal Church USA there are no fewer than seventeen hymn texts either written by Watts or to which he contributed a stanza or more. The same hymns have appeared in Protestant hymnals from the eighteenth century on and are among the best known and loved of the genre.

As the practice of religion in the Protestant world has moved out of the orbit of mainline denominational churches, hymns as such have become more or less relics in all but the most traditional Baptist and Holiness congregations, where, if they are sung at all, they tend be sung at prayer meetings and special services. Stand-alone congregations and mega-churches have turned by and large to what is called "Christian music" that features the ecclesiastical versions of torch songs, upbeat praise music with constantly repeated refrains. Often enough, congregation participants merely clap their hands or swing to and fro in their seats to the beat of such songs, or sing along whilst watching the projection of the words on large screens. Such music has entered the lives of both Roman Catholic and mainline Protestant churches as well, with "praise" and "folk" groups increasingly substituting for and even replacing organs and choirs as music leaders and performers.

A whole other genre of religious music is the so-called "Negro spiritual." Such spirituals and other hymns are in a class by themselves and will not be treated in this study. Some of them emerged from the slave communities of the ante-bellum South and lived on to assuage the pain caused by the criminal treatment of African Americans during Reconstruction right up to and including the Civil Rights movement and beyond. There is nothing quite like being part of a congregation made up predominantly of African Americans singing, for example, James Weldon Johnson's

Lift Every Voice and Sing or *Precious Lord, Take My Hand*. Hymns that scan well and are sung to memorable tunes tend to satisfy the *psyche* the way comfort food satisfies the *soma*.

A character in one of John P. Marquand's novels tells a person whom he has just met, "There's nothing like a good sound hymn to settle your stomach."[4] The most popular hymns have rhyming patterns and are provided with soprano, alto, tenor and bass lines. Their melodies are not difficult to sing. The sound a decent sized congregation is able to make from hymns thus equipped can produce that kind of satisfying feeling to which the Marquand character referred. A random check of the pages of three still-used hymnals of mainline Protestant denominations[5] shows that virtually every hymn follows one rhyming pattern or another, such as the following:

> O God of earth and altar, bow down and hear our cry,
> our earthy rulers falter, our people drift and die,
> the walls of gold entomb us, the swords of scorn divide,
> take not thy thunder from us, but take away our pride.[6]

Easy-to-follow meter together with rhyming lines help etch in memory a poignant text, especially when accompanied by an easy-to-sing, not yet hackneyed tune, much as the text above is most often sung to *King's Lynn*, an English melody adapted by Ralph Vaughan Williams.

By contrast the easy-to-follow and sing Sunday school hymn known as *Jesus Loves Me* is fundamentally annoying to anyone who appreciates decent poetry and a lilting score:

> Jesus loves me. This I know.
> For the Bible tells me so . . .

The hymns to be considered in this book come from many different traditions, times and necessities. Serious musicians see them on a spectrum from annoyingly simplistic to engagingly sublime with plenty somewhere near the middle. Each and all of them, though, emerged from cultural and religious experiences and tend to reflect the times in and conditions under which they were composed.

Chapter 1

North American Christianity
. . . in the Nineteenth and Twentieth Centuries

Once the dust of the Revolutionary War settled and the United States of America began to become itself, the populace of the new nation, now freed from the bonds of an established church, sought in various ways to try its wings in re-inventing what had been handed down to them as Separatists, Anglicans, and Methodists, among other expressions of what had been essentially European and British expressions of Protestant Christianity. Lutherans and Roman Catholics also began to organize as American presences on the public square.

Institutional religion and personal piety, even among deists and closet agnostics, remained important parts of the new nation's life. What had been known as the Church of England had quickly to change its identity inasmuch as many of its divines had opposed the revolution and separation from England. Because John and Charles Wesley had been Anglican priests before their dismissal from the established church, a good many American Anglicans defected to Methodism. A census-like count around 1820 reported that Anglicans in what is now North Carolina had dwindled to fewer than fifty members in the first decades of the nineteenth century.[7] Things improved modestly thereafter, and once the American church had its own bishops in the persons of Samuel Seabury of Connecticut and William White of Pennsylvania, the re-named Episcopal Church became a presence in the post-Revolutionary period. It would grow to an extent along the eastern seaboard and in the South, and would become a base of operations for the Confederacy after 1861, with several of its bishops made generals of the army of the Confederacy.

It was, however, American Methodism that reaped the early rewards. John Wesley was importuned in 1784 to ordain elders for a reformed version of Anglicanism along the lines of the discipline he and his brother had formed within but at the outer edges of the Church of England's orbit. Between 1784 and 1790, the number of Methodist adherents increased almost 400 percent. That added to the circuit-rider ministry made popular in England by the Wesleys; Methodism hit the frontier on horseback to spread the gospel, Paul Revere-like, "through every . . . village, and farm."[8]

The religion vended by the horseback preachers was a salvific one. As Wesley is reported to have said: "One condition, and only one, is required: a real desire to save the soul." He who by his own testimony "felt his heart strangely warmed" after evensong at Aldersgate Chapel one night in May 1738, having heard a lector read Luther's preface to Paul's Epistle to the Romans, wanted anyone and everyone to have such an experience.[9]

Thus, it was not a steely Calvinism Wesley and his followers brought to rural and frontier America, but a free-will, grace-filled doctrine of salvation worked out by the Dutch theologian Jacobus Arminius. It was a gentle but straight-ahead kind of Bible-based evangelicalism proceeding, as it were, from a warmed heart.

Withal, the sermons of the circuit riders were not often marked by a great deal of erudition, biblical or otherwise, but were filled with firm but gentle invitations to both accept and acquire holiness—accepting the proffered grace of the Protestant deity but reaching out to grasp it as well. Such preachments were characterized by a revivalist zeal that extended its influence so far as Yale University. Excited by a course of sermons given by Yale's president, Timothy Dwight, around 1802, the free-thinking faction among students yielded up a rash of conversions.

Revivals farther away from such institutions as Yale were characterized by a raw kind of emotionalism. But their settings were in new, largely uncharted territory with migrants moving through and sometimes moving in for short periods of time. Institutional religion did not immediately put down roots and erect buildings; thus, it was the open-air or tent revivals that served the purposes later undertaken by churches of various denominations.

To what extent such revivals were received more as entertainment than soul-saving vehicles is not known. But this much seems true, namely, that their emotionalism gave rise to the sentiments of many a hymn reflecting what systematic theologians would call simplistic interpretations of biblical texts and established doctrine.

On the rugged and unforgiving terrain of the rural frontier, life could be very difficult, especially for women and even more especially for women responsible for children. Their husbands, at best, labored from dawn to dusk to provide for their families and, at worst, gave in to the lure of the saloon and cheap liquor topped off by easy sex with prostitutes.

What women with husbands like the latter craved was gentleness and understanding, which they may not ordinarily have gotten from the men in their lives. The image of a savior "softly and tenderly"[10] calling to them from on high must have been a blessing. Hymns of the kind analyzed later in these pages were ready palliatives.

More and more as the nineteenth century got along, the Protestant and free-church movements emphasized the personage of Jesus, sometimes to the total exclusion of what theologians would call "God, the Father" and "God, the Holy Spirit." Just as the mid-to-late first-century communities of Jesus Judaism— the nascent church—focused attention on the Jesus figure first through the cosmic soteriology of Paul's "Christ Jesus"; secondly, through the narrative gospels' stories and sayings of Jesus of Nazareth; and finally, through the prism of the Gospel of John that presented the incarnate Jesus (cf. John 1:14) as the pre-existent divine *logos* (John 8:59: "Before Abraham was, I am"; NRSV).

That same Jesus emerged in the sermons and Sunday school lessons of nineteenth-century North American Christianity as an almost palpable human being extending comfort, friendship, and surcease especially to those for whom life was one struggle after the other as they attempted to eke out livings in the impersonal environment of economically unforgiving cities or as they tried to homestead the land and extract crops from it, all the while fighting drought, insect invasions, and brutal winters.

The once-popular television series *Little House on the Prairie* is a highly romanticized version of what rural life was like during the period it depicts. Families lived at great distances from one another in terms of what, besides their feet, they had for transportation: horse and wagon or just a horse. Even as towns sprang up along early railroad lines moving inexorably westward, those farming the land or raising cattle were generally far from the civilization, such as it might have been, of such towns. To compensate for the isolation, families banded together to found what came to be known as "section schools" named for the township divisions in which they were built—often enough as the one-room schoolhouses well known to oater film watchers. In such schools were frequently ensconced the eldest daughters of nearby farmers, who not only had learned to read and write but could do basic arithmetic and were thought, perhaps, not to be prime candidates for marriage—hence, the term "school marm." Such was basic education for those children who could be spared from the labors of hard-scrabble farms.

Migrants westward across the continent brought with them memories of what it was like to go to church, hear sermons, and sing hymns. Learned clergy were few and far between out on the land of the expanding nation. Sometimes in the very one-room building that served as a schoolhouse Monday through Friday (except in planting and harvest seasons and otherwise when the snow was too deep or the storms too fierce), ad hoc congregations gathered twice each Sunday (a service after the morning barn chores, another before those of the evening) to hear the gospel preached by a man with an audible voice, who could read what the Bible said and regurgitate it with acceptable embellishment and fervor. Such a man, drafted from the ruck of his less attractive peers, was most likely unacquainted with and uncaring, say, of the plight of the Jebusites, was unable to pick up the clues in Genesis that the text was not about when the world was created or how, and was apt to be more interested in the sound of his own voice than what it actually articulated, yet became the source of all religious wisdom for his congregation.

If the hymn texts that became popular in that era are accepted as evidence, it would be fair to suggest that "gentle Jesus, meek and mild"[11] was the likely subject for many sermons and that the women in those congregations—who, then as now, usually outnumbered men in the pews—embraced that Jesus as a surrogate for the men of their dreams. Filial relationships of men with their mothers and marriage with their spouses could and did produce emotion-laden hymns as well. Freed from the formalism of high church liturgy and the demanding sermons of learned clergy, Christianity on the North American continent developed a repertoire of hymnody that would be sung well into the twenty-first century by those for whom the piety of the past provides a buffer against the problems of the present.

Death as experienced close-up in mid-nineteenth- and twentieth-century America as a result of the War Between the States and World War I had a profound influence on hymn writing. War deaths, especially in the South between 1861 and 1865, were higher than the cumulative total of all armed conflicts from the Revolution through the Korean war. The so-called Civil War took young men in the bloom of their youth and ground them into meal. Corpses were shoveled into mass graves, not out of disregard for their sacrifice or their survivors' sensibilities but because of the rightful fear of epidemic, so widespread were the dead. Thomas Wolfe accounted for the gore of it all about as well as anyone in his short story "Chickamauga":

> I don't know how many men got killed. I don't know which side lost the most. I only know you could have walked across the dead men without settin' foot upon the ground. . . . I have been in some big battles, I can tell you. I've seen strange things

and been in bloody fights. But the biggest fight that I was ever in—the bloodiest battle anyone has ever fought—was at Chickamauga in that cedar thicket—at Chickamauga Creek in that great war.[12]

It was not only the wounds sustained in battle but the sketchy medical treatment to which the wounded had access. Amputations were done perforce without modern anesthesia: a pull or two on a whiskey bottle and a piece of hardwood between the teeth. The first researcher who developed the modern understanding of sepsis—Ignaz Semmelweis—died in 1865, and his work was done entirely in Vienna. The keen observations of Louis Pasteur and Joseph Lister came too late for tens of thousands of Civil War casualties, who died not from their initial wounds but from the bacterially contaminated surgeons' hands, gloves, and instruments. Blood and plenty of it was an unforgettable image of the war, and it is no accident that blood would become a frequently used word in post-bellum hymns, namely, "the blood of Jesus" that one hymnist called "the cleansing flood."

Withal, in a world supposedly presided over by a benevolent deity, the 1861–65 war was pretty hard for survivors to take. Since God the Father was remote from everyday experience, there was a natural reaching out for the one person of the Holy Trinity who, supposedly, actually walked on Earth and, as a human being, had relationships with other human beings, and further was depicted as suffering an excruciating death by crucifixion. Maybe He could understand, and even though He had supposedly returned to the heaven whence He came, the faithful could reach out to Him in prayer.

Between the late eighteenth century and the end of the War Between the States, America had evolved from an officially secular state to being "a Christian nation." That evolution describes an interesting arc in the country's history, which would bring Christian theology and piety to the center of national life.

Virtually all of the parties principal to the founding of the United States had some form of Christianity in their near or distant backgrounds—mostly seventeenth- and eighteenth-century English Protestantism varying from the High Church faction of Anglicanism to Cromwellian and post-Cromwellian dissent. Seventeenth-century Anglicanism was a pretty arid desert. Parish ministers were generally not very devout, and religion was a matter of form for most of them and their congregations—which, by the way, were comprised of wealthy landowners. The church was the state, and the state was the church. The treatment of dissenters ranged from ex-communication to public whipping. It wasn't so much theological orthodoxy that was the issue. The issue was never doubting the power of Mother Church that was the spiritual part of the monarchy.

Withal, the language and underlying philosophy of most literate English men and women was to be found in the literature, written and spoken, of the Church of England—however much in secret or not-so-secret dissent a person was. It is therefore technically correct to say that the United States of America was founded by Christian persons. Thomas Paine, of course, had long since departed anything close to Christianity, and was shunned even by deists and other dissenters because his criticism of Christianity, its doctrines, and its institutions was as scathing as it was uncomfortably true. Paine and Thomas Jefferson were brothers in the bond, but Jefferson had to keep Paine at arm's length whilst he served in the Washington cabinet and later as president, lest his politics and policies would be compromised by public knowledge of their shared friendship and skepticism.

What few references exist to religion in America's founding documents seem self-consciously deist in nature, that is, a willingness to make oblique references to a source-orderer of the material world but not to commit the nation to some school of theology. It is instructive to know and to notice that neither the word "God" nor the word "church" occurs anywhere in the Constitution, and the words "religious" and "religion" appear only in two places: Article VI, which prohibits a religious test for election to any public office, and the First Amendment of the Bill of Rights, which prohibits Congress from enacting laws to establish as official any particular religion or to interfere with the free exercise of whatever religion or religions may be the wont of people living under the protection of said Constitution.

It was left to Jefferson to coin the phrase "separation of church and state." What did he mean by that? We will let him speak for himself as we quote the pertinent passage of a letter he wrote to the Baptist ministers of Danbury, Conn. on January 1, 1802 in response to their pointed inquiry as to whether the laws of the new nation granted religionists the right to worship as they would, or whether said laws merely recognized that right. Wrote Jefferson:

> Believing with you that religion is a matter which lies solely between Man & his God, that he owes account to none other for his faith or his worship, that the legitimate powers of government reach actions only, & not opinions, I contemplate with sovereign reverence that act of the whole American people which declared that their legislature should "make no law respecting an establishment of religion, or prohibiting the free exercise thereof," thus building a wall of separation between Church & State. Adhering to this expression of the supreme will of the nation in behalf of the rights of conscience, I shall see with sincere satisfaction the progress of those sentiments which tend to restore to man all his natural rights, convinced he has no natural right in opposition to his social duties.[13]

Jefferson's language is that of a politician. He did not wish to bring Baptist obloquy upon his head, and so, as you heard, his words were exquisitely chosen not to offend. He did not say straight-out that he was a believer. He used the word "God" but modified by the personal possessive pronoun "his," leaving the careful reader to figure that "his" did not mean "mine" or "ours." And it is in that careful distinction, more than the much-quoted and usually misunderstood phrase "separation of church and state," that the significance of Jefferson's letter lies. He was saying, "Look, you can worship whatever you conceive your God to be. Your neighbor may believe his dog is his god. So be it. He can worship his dog as god, and you can worship whatever you imagine god is."

One has to look carefully to get that meaning. That, though, is the nub of the issue. Insofar as Jefferson and many others like him among the founders were concerned, religions, their gods, and their rituals were to be permitted, encouraged even, in America, but religions, gods, and rituals were personal matters and could not be incorporated into government or governance. Could not, that is, be established. So America to Jefferson and his founder-colleagues was not a Christian nation, not even a religious nation collectively, even though various Christian churches would go on to flourish along with, eventually, every manner of religion.

No event or series of events in the history of American religion is of more significance than what literature of the period calls "the Great Awakening" of the 1730s that lasted into the 1740s. For reasons that had to do with the rustic and its wild uncertainty, the absence of large cities and of a grounding culture, a fierce brand of religion rushed in to the vacuum. Randall Balmer, a scholar of religion and its ideas, says it was "a massive revival of religion that swept through the Atlantic colonies in the middle decades of the eighteenth century, and it introduced to American society a peculiar strain of evangelicalism that remains America's folk religion to this day."[14] However, this book explores that very evangelicalism as it was expressed in the quintessential American hymns that were composed by devotees of the same—hymns that are sung to this day in many a church, despite the intellectually questionable theology they convey in verse that is often doggerel and sometimes even execrable doggerel. That brand of religion came as close to being an entity of establishment as anything down to this day. It was headlined by such great orators as Jonathon Edwards and George Whitefield, whose sermons caused women to swoon and men to sweat. Hell was an ever-present possibility and people converted and re-converted trying to cover all the bases to keep themselves from perdition.

What saved the nation from an establishment of that religious expression was Whitefield himself—a Methodist who did not need a church edifice in which to preach his gospel. He took to field and forest, village square and other open places, to preach his revival. This had the effect of atomizing the movement and

making it a matter more private and personal, and less orga-
nizational. But, as Balmer says, that evangelicalism is with us
still, only now that the nation has been urbanized not only
geographically but spatially by television and the Internet, orga-
nizationalism is present even among independent churches and
congregations in which people of like mind make or find affirma-
tion of their beliefs.

The point is that colonial America was not only religious but
hyper-religious at what we might call the grassroots. In that
sense, it can be said that what was in the making was "a Christian
nation," in that it was not a Hindu nation, not a Buddhist nation,
not a Jewish nation. Those swept up in the Great Awakening
were culturally already oriented to Christianity if only by virtue
of whence their forebears had come. They were caught up in a
fad, shall we say, because if they were nothing else, Edwards
and Whitefield were great entertainment. They were the earlier
equivalent of the Barnum & Bailey circus come to town in rural
Iowa in 1890 before the days of movies, radio, television, the
Internet or e-mail, Tweeting and texting. That made religion a
commodity. More and more preachers came to town and set
up their tents and soapboxes. People had choices, and favorites
appeared.

It became a free-market kind of deal that was precisely the sort
of thing the framers of the Constitution had in mind. Let religion
flourish if it could. Keep it a private matter of the heart. Let those
who were drawn to it embrace it. Let those who wanted a different message seek it out. Let those content with no message at
all, alone. James Madison, an ardent separationist, had predicted
that total freedom of religion would so decentralize the phenomenon that the idea of establishment could never occur to its pro-
ponents. Indeed, the Baptists were known from the beginning as
advocating separation of church and state.

Return for the moment to the mid-to-late seventeenth century
in colonial America. The grassroots, if we can describe the farmer
or the artisan that way, were Christian, and many of them serious
about it due to the Great Awakening. Their immediate descendants followed that same mindset.

They fought in the War of Revolution, hated the British on principle, refused to brook interference with their religious preferences; they also were not keen on the idea that the country of which they were becoming citizens and even voters in this new experiment in democracy would be atheist in nature. However, the grassroots were not in charge. It was an elite, the nascent country's intelligentsia, that wrote the Declaration of Independence and the Constitution and served as leaders in the new American government. It would take a backwoodsman like Andrew Jackson to emerge as the nation's first populist President. The grassroots may have remembered the wording of the Declaration of Independence that did mention the words "God" and "creator." Jefferson and his fellow authors of that 1776 document made reference to a deity in the phrase concerning the idea that all are created equal and are "endowed by their Creator with certain inalienable rights." Also in a preceding sentence are the words: "The laws of nature and of nature's God." Jefferson was not a believer, but, as we have noted, he was a politician, and must have known that to connect "inalienable rights" with a Creator would speak to the piety of the people. He must also have realized that to reference the laws of nature he ought to allude to a deity behind said nature and its laws. That, however, is all the masses got of religion in the Declaration of Independence, and they wound up with none in the Constitution. Again, the framers were not the masses. They were the educated elite.

As the end of the eighteenth century hove into view and America was on the threshold of being born, it would have been accurate to say that it was collectively a Christian nation, if only because whatever religious orientation people had was Christian, even if it was as sketchy as Jefferson's and others of the elite. But as elites often do, the first American elite acted on its own instincts and decided to do for the People what the elite decided was right and proper, and did not ask for a plebiscite. The elite decided to create, basically, a secular state with the freedom of religion, which, by logical extension, provided freedom from religion. But religion will out. Amanda Porterfield, a scholar of the history of religion and politics, points out that religion at the very end of the eighteenth century and the beginning of the nine-teenth became a means of enforcing political visions and agenda through what can only be called "mind control."[15]

Nevertheless, on paper America became a secular, that is to say, not a religious nation. It was the Mother of All Paradoxes: a totally anti-democratic process, like a parent making his kid eat spinach because it is good for him. It would not happen today. Yet, can you imagine an America without the freedom of (even from) religion? Can you imagine America without the wall of separation between church and state and, some would say, re-ligion and governance? The First Amendment made it possible for Joseph Smith to invent Mormonism and for it essentially to own one of the fifty states. It made it possible for Mary Baker Eddy to invent Christian Science, which is, any way you look at it, an oxymoron. It even paved the way for the invention of the Black Muslim movement which has saved the day for millions of African Americans. It made it possible for Central, Southern, and Eastern Europeans to bring their various Catholicisms to this country and to form a Diaspora among ethnic communities in what was essentially a Protestant country. It made it possible for German and Russian Ashkenazi Jews to immigrate and to build their Temples and synagogues.

The events above serve as prologue to what is known as the Second Great Awakening (ca. 1800–40) in American religion— American Christianity, really. It was almost the singular creation of an evangelist known as Charles Finney of Connecticut, trained in the law but called, he believed, to preach the gospel. Finney had accumulated considerable doubt about the Calvinism of his predecessors. They had taught people that they were entirely dependent on divine disposition toward them, which they could neither create nor destroy. Some were called to eternal life, oth-ers to damnation. And since one couldn't know until the roll was called up yonder, it behooved him or her to do exactly as the preacher said. Talk about mind control.

Finney contradicted that idea and told people hungry for an easier way that they could actually earn eternal salvation, and that through the simple matter of belief. All they needed to do was to confess and then espouse the idea that merely believing that the biblical Jesus in his death and resurrection offered everlasting life to those who would simply believe that and embrace it in their hearts. People converted to that brand of religion by the tens of thousands. Gone was the nagging doubt about whether one was of the elect or of the damned. Finney put the whole proposition in the hands of the individual, much as Henry Ford's Models T and A made it possible for the individual to drive where he wanted, when he wanted, and at the speed he wanted. That pretty much sums up what evangelical Christianity had become, say, by the time of the War Between the States, which introduced the specter of death to the American grassroots as nothing had before. More than a half million dead and dying left an indelible mark on the consciousness of America, Yankee or Rebel. It was death considered to have been random and undeserved. Out of that came a piety that would become a new evangelicalism, rich with sentiment and individual hopes.

The era that followed upon the Civil War was one of enormous expansion. The railroads together with the Industrial Revolution burst upon the American scene. The South rose up in high dudgeon against its miserable defeat and made the life of former slaves worse than before their Emancipation in an era known now by the odd name of "Reconstruction" (1863–77). Protestant Christianity in the beaten South became a venue for righteous indignation and a rough-hewn piety that emphasized the rights of people to decide for themselves about social issues. The Bible was mined for justification of oppression of African Americans and continued sedition. The Confederate Flag, actually a symbol of humiliation and defeat, became, in the white church, second only to the cross as the symbol of eventual victory.

As the nation expanded westward, that kind of jut-jawed determination became a central theme. It was in such venues that the longing for the old-time religion, whatever it may have been, was repeated and repeated. The learning of professors of the new land-grant colleges and universities was spurned for the old verities of the Good Book. Trouble was that the Industrial Revolution was turning the nation from rusticity to urbanity, and more and more people left the frontier to the depleted buffalo herds and the railroads blasting through to the West Coast. People came to cities, but with their religious sentiments intact. Waiting for them were people like Dwight Moody, of the Moody Bible Institute, a center of evangelicalism.

American colleges and universities were playing catch-up in the late nineteenth and early twentieth centuries as their science faculties had to absorb the epoch-making observations and hypotheses of Charles Darwin and the effect they had on the intellectuals' understanding of the world. Not that Darwin had spoken or written the first word on the idea that the biblical account of creation was incredible. Darwin merely pulled together in a very convincing way the various threads and skeins of observation, research, and hypothesizing so that the study of the biosphere was forever changed. Not only science faculties but those of philosophy and religion also had to adjust their approach to the greater questions. What we call "higher criticism" or the "historical-critical" approach to such religious texts as the Hebrew Bible and the appendices to it called the New Testament arose primarily in early nineteenth-century Germany with the work of Julius Wellhausen and others whose research and analysis demonstrated that the Pentateuch was not a monolithic text but a crazy quilt of several different traditions from disparate times and circumstances, but which were trying to tell the same kinds of stories.

That may not sound like much from our twenty-first century perspective, but it had a world-shaking affect upon those who were preparing to become clergyman and as well upon those already in congregations whose members had for generations heard and responded to a far different approach to what they believed were sacred texts. Now here were scholars analyzing its bits and pieces and showing conclusively that if the Bible was the Word of God, there must have been many gods doing the speaking. And, what's more, their stories varied. The new approach put biblical literature in the same class as other literature: the plays of William Shakespeare and the poetry of John Milton, for example. Biblical texts were now studied not as the dictated Word of God but as the labors of poets and philosophers. They were studied as historical documents. Research was done on their vocabularies and syntax for clues to the purpose and provenance. That was a huge sea-change, but it was rejected by many American clergy and was not permitted to be taught in many seminaries. As a result, the congregations served by graduates of such seminaries and lesser bible schools did not have the benefit of the better scholarship. Society at large caught on to the idea that, as Ira Gershwin had put it in the libretto of "Porgy and Bess, "the things you're liable to read in the Bible, they ain't necessarily so." Graduate schools of theology not bound to denominational necessity began to teach the higher criticism, resulting in an unstoppable force headed for an immovable object—what was known in the early twentieth century as "the fundamentalist controversy." Another facet of this upset was the social gospel movement in which predominantly Protestant clergy shifted the focus of the church's attention from theology to ethics. Washington Gladden and Frank Mason North, both of whom wrote hymns discussed in Part II below, were pioneers of that movement. Their latter-day successor was Harry Emerson Fosdick of the noted hymn *God of Grace, and God of Glory*, also discussed in Part II.

Fosdick was at the center of the fundamentalist controversy. Many fundamentalists were concerned with the idea of American exceptionalism and manifest destiny. If, as some of the early seventeenth-century colonialists believed, America was really a second "promised land" and God had spared the lives of those who weathered the Atlantic crossing to claim it, then America must be a Christian nation, a special place and people created for the purpose of showing forth the glory of God. A Bible taken uncritically and spared the rigors of textual and historical investigation would yield exactly such conclusions. The idea was that Israel had failed in its mission to become the chosen people. Now it was the people and the nation that would become the United

States that was that land and that people. But it became difficult to make that point with any kind of intellectual credibility if the Bible was just another collection of human-generated texts, and not the literal Word of God.

The higher criticism also threatened the various churches' control over their constituents. If the guys up front in the pulpits did not have the eternal word of God in their hands when they preached their sermons, why would you take them seriously or fear their admonitions and scoldings? A new brand of clergy was coming down the pike; in particular, Fosdick, whose name was a household word in the 1920s and '30s and beyond, forged the way toward a rational religion. In so doing Fosdick found himself in the gun sights of the fundamentalist wing of the denomination in which he was serving at the time. The reactionaries, sensing the peril in the shift in authority, sought to lead people back to a hidebound traditionalism, denying the discoveries and observations of science and insisting upon the literal acceptance of every passage in the Bible. Often with evangelical fundamentalists, it's all or nothing. Believe the whole thing, or be damned. It was just that attitude that gave the nation one of its by-now famous circus freak-shows. I speak of the trial of Tennessee high school biology teacher, John T. Scopes, in which the then most famous fundamentalist of all, William Jennings Bryan, played a major role. The state of Tennessee was about as backward a place in the 1920s as parts of Texas are today. The Tennessee legislature, at the behest of fundamentalist church leaders, enacted a law making it a misdemeanor to teach evolutionary biology in the state's public schools because Darwin was obviously wrong in his conclusion that Homo sapiens was an evolved life form with simian ancestors. That idea was repugnant to those who had been taught to believe that the Bible was the first and last truth about the world as it was. To think even for an instant that Jesus Christ was the descendant of an ape made them physically ill. And furthermore, James Ussher, a Church of Ireland Archbishop in the mid-seventeenth century—and a prolific scholar by standards of the time—published a chronology that Ussher said established the time and date of the creation as the night preceding Sunday, 23 October 4004 BCE.

Thus, there would not have been time for apes to have evolved by the time Christ was born, so Darwin was wrong and should be ignored inasmuch he was dead by the 1920s and couldn't be burned at the stake. The Tennessee fundamentalists did not want their children's minds contaminated by such heresy. If the Bible was wrong about creation, what could it be right about? That was the big threat to those who thought they lived and moved and had their being in God's own country governed by God's own Bible. Into that Potemkin Village of innocence and ignorance came the American Civil Liberties Union to challenge the anti-Darwin law. The ACLU recruited Scopes to make a test case: He taught one day's worth of evolutionary biology and was immediately cited for violating state law and a trial was in the works. Bryan came to support the prosecution. Clarence Darrow came to aid in Scopes' defense. A true clash of the titans, only Darrow got the best of Bryan when he got him to admit that a day in the Genesis text didn't necessarily mean a mere twenty-four hours. In fact, a biblical day could mean any length of time. In a sense, the roof fell in on Bryan with that admission, and the sun seemed to set on fundamentalism for good. Actually, it did not. Scopes was convicted and fined 100 dollars for his trouble, which the ACLU paid, and the circus left Dayton, Tennessee, but not before having been the butt of jokes in newspapers all over the United States and Europe. The ACLU claimed victory on principle and pronounced Bryan's kind of ideology dead as a doornail. That was incorrect. Bryan's kind of ideology was broader and deeper than either Darrow or the ACLU knew. What it did was to retreat almost into hibernation—but not for long. You do not beat up a true believer with impunity. A book by Edward J. Larson entitled *Summer of the Gods: The Scopes Trial and America's Continuing Debate Over Science and Religion* is a dependable resource for details about the trial.

The fundamentalists, as yet not well organized, went home and licked their wounds, but were mad as hell. The Scopes trial took place in the summer of 1925 at just about the time radio was beginning to tie people together in a smaller but still significant way along the lines of today's Internet. Among the first types to take advantage of the airwaves were fundamentalist preachers in an effort to expand their ministries. What they were doing in today's terminology was networking. Federations formed, and they went on shelling peas in the moonlight waiting for the day they could emerge to take America back for God and the Bible. As more and more people in more and more places had radios and stayed up later at night to hear music and voices from far away, fundamentalist preachers became increasingly well-known—not among city folk, most of whom thought that stuff silly, but among farmers out on the Plains and in the small towns of mid-America, where the simplistic message of the preachers received a warm welcome because it reiterated the old red-white-and-blue verities, strict morality and unchanging beliefs.

It was in such an environment that the pietistic gospel hymns became Christian "national anthems."

Chapter 2

The Jesus of the Bible and Creeds

The existence of a single "Jesus" is not supported by historical data. Moreover, the various Jesuses we meet in the hymns of the nineteenth and twentieth century are not always the same Jesuses we meet in the gospels. That is so partly because the Jesus figure—or figures—are opaque. The stories about them fail to meet the requirements of history. In the eye of the uncatechized observer they appear to be myths or at some level to partake in mythology. One cannot in this age accept uncritically and without rationalization such stories as the feeding of the five thousand on a scant supply of five loaves and two fish, the magical healing of people with various maladies, the *deus ex machina* feature of the Road to Emmaus narrative, the spectral appearances of resurrected Jesuses and his ascension as reported in Luke 24:51.

The Jesus character is limned differently—sometimes much differently—just in the four canonical gospels. The Jesus of the Gospel of Mark, thought to be the first attempt to organize the extant pieces of first-century oral tradition, is an iconoclast portrayed almost as looking in a provocative way for trouble with the religious authorities, such as his altercation with the Pharisees over picking grain to eat on the Sabbath (2:23–28). Mark includes no infancy narrative and no allusion to one. Mark's gospel concludes at chapter 16:8 with the odd statement that the women who had come to the tomb left confused and told no one about what they had seen—and not seen—"because they were afraid indeed [ἐφοβουντο γάρ]." Mark is missing some of

the better known sayings attributed to the Jesuses of Matthew
and Luke, most of which appear to have come out of the collection known as Quelle—or the so-called "Q" document, *quelle*
being the German term for "source."

The Gospel of Matthew, which followed Mark's version by as
many as fifteen years, depicts a Jesus who was interested in connecting traditional Judaism with his own emerging movement.
The truth of the matter is that those of the emerging movement in
the years following the destruction of the Jerusalem Temple in 70
CE were trying to connect the tradition represented by the Temple
to their departure from it. Fully nine separate events in Matthew
are tied to prophetic predictions found in the text of the Hebrew
Bible (see 1:22–23, 2:15, 2:17, 2:23, 4:14–16, 12:17–21, 13:35, 21:4–5,
and 27:9–10). As if to emphasize the point, Matthew begins with
a genealogical tracing of Jesus back through David to Abraham.
The Jesus of Matthew is a law-giver in the tradition of Moses,
as seen in 5:1–7:29, a compendium of sayings attributed to Jesus
which can be found in parallel instances in Luke. Matthew is
heavy on judgment and light on grace. The sheep-and-goats metaphor of Matt 25:31–36 features wailing and gnashing of teeth.

Matthew is the first gospel to deal directly with the resurrection story, but in a very careful way, namely, depicting a) the
women going to the tomb, b) the occurrence of "a great earth-
quake" for audio and an angel descending from on high for
visual, c) the guards fainting in their astonishment, d) the angel
telling the women Jesus "has been raised" and that they should
tell the disciples get themselves hence to Galilee where Jesus will
meet them, e) the women suddenly encountering Jesus, evidently
falling down before him and grasping his feet and f) the appearance of Jesus on the Galilean highlands where he commissions
the disciples to become baptizing apostles, promising to be with
them as long as the world remained.

The Gospel of Luke is clearly dependent on the Markan and
Matthean texts that came before it. Luke's Jesus is not connected
so firmly to traditional Judaism. Luke's genealogy ties his Jesus
not only to David and Abraham but to Adam, making Jesus a

universal character in a universal drama that includes but is not limited to Israel. The Lukan infancy narrative gives more ink to Mary than Matthew's and recognizes in the persons of the shepherds that Jesus is on the side of the poor and lower economic classes. Women are elevated to a new plateau of importance as depicted in 7:36–50, 8:3, and 10:38–42. The gospel written in refined Greek seems to be intended for a Gentile audience, as scarce attention is paid to texts of the Hebrew Bible. Luke's Jesus is the avatar of compassion and gentleness. The parable of the prodigal son (15:1–32) is Luke's signature instance of unconditional forgiveness. The Road to Emmaus story (24:13–35) is a sweet grace note in the narrative, but Jesus is only one of three main characters in it. He is depicted as teaching and sharing, quickly appearing and quickly disappearing—the resurrection and ascension stories presaged.

Though not mentioned by name, Jesus is introduced to the reader of the Gospel of John in an entirely new way. The prologue to the gospel is the closest its writer gets to an infancy narrative. Cast in terms of Greek philosophy, the one who becomes Jesus by verse 29 of chapter one is said to be the *logos* ("Word") which means "that by which the inner thought is expressed," or "the main thing" (as in the German *ding an sich*) and is understood to denote the all-encompassing wisdom and power of the deity. John says this "Word" was *en archay*, meaning not so much "in the beginning" as beyond and before time, and that the Word was what God is and was the agency through which everything came to be.

It is from that platform that the fourth gospel goes on to depict a larger-than-life human figure standing above other human beings in grand singularity and uniqueness. This Jesus is not only the agency of all creation but capable of transforming water into wine (2:1–11); he tells a Samaritan woman the whole story of her life, having never met her or known about her (4:16–18); he heals in an instant a man who had been lame for thirty-eight years (5:5–9); he presides over another instance of a mass feeding with a sparse lunch (6:1–13); he restores sight to a blind man at the pool of Siloam (9:1–41), taking a lot of guff from the Pharisees who objected to that work being done on the Sabbath; he declines to let death have the upper hand at Bethany and in an act reminiscent of *elohim* speaking light into being (Gen 1:3) summons a three-days' dead Lazarus from his stinking tomb back to life; he sets forth propositions in several "I am" statements also reminding one of Exod 3:14 ("I AM THAT I AM"); he is not only raised from the dead but continues to be here and there, materializing through locked doors and on the beach at dawn (20:19, 20:26, and 21:1).

The Gospel of Thomas, part of the Nag Hammadi trove found in 1945, appears in Coptic but probably originated in Greek (if not Aramaic). It is a collection of sayings attributed to Jesus and may come from as early as 50–60 CE. The Jesus revealed in the Thomas collection of sayings is an epigrammatist, teaching by the first-century version of the sound-bite. Many of the 114 sayings appear in some form or another in the synoptic gospels. There is no hint that the speaker of the sayings is anything other than the speaker of the sayings. No material that might be considered biographical in any sense is to be found in Thomas

Likewise Paul's epistles provide very little in the way of accounting for any Jesus of history. He is most often referred to as "Christ Jesus" by Paul, is never allowed to speak for himself in any saying, save possibly 1 Cor 11:23ff. There Paul repeats the words the synoptic evangelists put on Jesus' lips in their depictions of the Last Supper.

The longer one lives with the New Testament gospels and their individual texts, the more one spots and wonders over the differences among them with respect to their portrayals of Jesus. It is not difficult to become conditioned to believe that any first-century figure with the name "Jesus" is the one and only Jesus, and, moreover, that there was only one Jesus as there is only one God and that Jesus is, as the Bible says, the only Son of that God.

The facts are tougher than that. "Jesus" is a name transliterated from New Testament Greek, Ἰησοῦς, which in turn is an approximation of the Aramaic *Yeshuah*, typically written in English as *Joshua.* By no means was *Yeshuah* an uncommon name for a male child in first-century Palestine. Variations on the name appear as Jesus Barabbas, Jesus Justus, Jesus Son of Sirach. Flavius Josephus references the following: Jesus son of Phabat, Jesus son of Ananus, Jesus son of Sapphias, Jesus brother of Onias, Jesus son of Gamaliel, Jesus a priest after Ananus, Jesus son of Damneus, Jesus son of Gamala, Jesus son of Nun, Jesus son of Saphat, Jesus son of Thebuthus and Jesus son of Josedek.

Since the gospels are not historical digests but rather written versions of oral proclamations, one would expect that the "Jesus" featured in each document was based somehow on an actual character or on characters who lived and enjoyed some kind of limited prominence during the first third of the first century CE. It is disturbing to some to suggest that the Jesus, say of Thomas, was a different person than the Jesus, say, of John. A compelling exploration of just that idea can be found in Elaine Pagels' book *Beyond Belief: The Secret Gospel of Thomas.*[16] Suffice it to say that if there existed from circa 4 BCE to circa 27 CE the very person or persons called "Jesus" in the four canonical gospels and in sixteen extant non-canonical gospel texts, we have little dependable information about him or them. His or their existence is not well attested outside the Bible. Flavius Josephus mentions a "Jesus Christ" but once, in *The Antiquities of the Jews* (18.3.1ff). The Roman historians Tacitus and Suetonius each make mention of a "Chrestus," referring, it seems, to the person or character prominent in the preaching of early Christianity.

It seems best for those who are serious about information as opposed to opinion or blind faith to accept the fact that the Jesus of Christianity is more a character of myth than a figure of history.

～

The Jesus of church creeds resembles hardly at all the one depicted in the texts of synoptic gospels, though one can glimpse the lineaments of John 1:1–18 expressed in the Nicene Creed. Otherwise, the assumption of the creeds is that there was but one Jesus on whom the whole of the Christian belief is predicated. If

the Nicene Creed were the only extant document of Christian antiquity, Jesus would appear to have been a scarcely known figure
woven here and there in a verbal tapestry of doctrine rather than
the human being variously depicted by the writers of the canonical gospels. By contrast, if the Gospel of Thomas were the only
early document we possessed, the Jesus of the Christian religion
would appear to resemble such a figure as Hillel the Elder (d. 10
CE), who was known for his dispensing of wisdom and ethical
philosophy.

The Nicene Creed makes Jesus the second person of the Trinity
and proclaims him

> the only Son of God,   1
> eternally begotten of the Father,
> God from God, Light from Light, true God from true God,
>   begotten not made, of one Being with the Father.
> Through him all things were made.
> For us and for our salvation he came down from heaven:
> by the power of the Holy Spirit he became incarnate from   6
>   the Virgin Mary
> and was made man.
> For our sake he was crucified
> under Pontius Pilate;
> he suffered death and was buried.
> On the third day he rose again   11
> in accordance with the Scriptures;
> he ascended into heaven
> and is seated at the right hand of the Father.
> He will come again in glory to judge the living and
>   the dead
> and his kingdom shall have no end.   16

Below, we shall search the scriptures for their warrant of such
proclamations, remembering that the biblical documents are
fragmentary in nature, seem not to have been created as support
for a systematic theology and, in fact, defy systemization as they
proceed out of nearly a millennium's worth of human history, out

of many varying cultures, in at least three languages, reflecting political and economic conflicts. The Bible is composed of poetry, mythology, legalities, liturgical rubrics, attempts to remember or create history, and so on. Nevertheless, the Christian church treats the collection known as the Bible as its point and frame of reference for the establishment and maintenance of its belief system. The major pieces of that system include:

1 *The only Son of God.* The primary text that backs up that proclamation occurs in John 1:1–18 and in particular this sentence: "And the Word became flesh and lived among us, and we have seen his glory as of a father's only son." That is an out-and-out proclamation founded on no known information, but it has been uncritically accepted as truth by millions of Christians over the past two thousand years.

2 *Eternally begotten of the Father.* "Eternally begotten" suggests that Jesus' status as the only Son of God is a dynamic, rather than a static thing. He is always being begotten. If that is not metaphor, I do not know what it is.

3 *Light from Light, true God from true God, begotten not made, of one Being with the Father.* Again one must look to the Prologue to the Gospel according to John for warrant. So far, this "Word" about to be made flesh does not look very human, as in the Jesus who chose to ignore the Syro-Phoenician woman and her pressing need (Mark 7:25–30 // Matt 15:21–28).

4 See John 1:10.

5 See Rom 5:6ff.

6 See Matt 1:18–25, Luke 1:26–38.

7 If Jesus was born of a woman, he would be human (man).

8–10 All four canonical gospels provide accounts of Jesus' crucifixion, with Luke mentioning that the execution included two criminals, with the clear implication that Jesus was considered a criminal by the executing authority.

9 While none of the canonical gospels provides an eyewitness account of the resurrection (see GPet 10:39–42), the resurrection is assumed. Mark's version is the most opaque,

ending abruptly as it does at 16:8 with the women who have been depicted as seeing an empty tomb telling no one "because they were afraid."

12 See Ps 16:10, Luke 25:25–27, and 1 Cor 15:4.

13 See Luke 24:51 and Acts 1:9–11.

14 See Ps 110:1, Matt 26:64, Acts 7:56, and Heb 1:3.

15 See Matt 16:27, 16:24–30, 16:25–31, 26:64; John 14:3; Acts 10:42, 17:3; Col 3:4; 1 Thess 4:16; and 1 Pet 4:5.

16 See Ps 145:13; Luke 1:33; John 18:36; 2 Tim 4:1, 18; and Rev 11:15.

In short, the Jesus of the hymn texts under consideration in this book resembles neither the figure confessed in the creed nor the one referenced in the biblical texts that lie at the base of the creedal affirmations. The Jesus of the creeds is a far cry from the "Savior who stands at the door of your heart" of Ina Dudley Ogden's verse, or the Jesus who "whispers sweet and low" in L.B. Bridges' hymn, or C. Austin Miles' Jesus who "walks with me" in the garden and "talks with me, and . . . tells me I am his own."

Part II
The Jesus of the Hymns

What follows are hymn texts that depict the Jesus figure in various ways that do not reflect much, or sometimes any, of its biblical and creedal depictions. Line by line, verse by verse, we will apply the process of exegesis to each hymn text, noting the provenance of the hymn where it can be known, what facts can be known about its author or authors, and the circumstances under which it was composed. This latter consideration may be the most important part of exegesis, that is, trying to figure out what prompted a text, what was going on in the life of the author as well as in the times in which he or she composed it. In my work with the canonical gospels and the Gospel of Thomas, I have tried always to ask what political, economic and social realities obtained, for example, in the Syrian communities out of which it is more or less accepted that Matthew emerged. I have gone so far as to hypothesize that the aforementioned gospels belong to the study of history. I have several times successfully taught a course called The Gospels as Church History.

The purpose of this study is to discern what authors fabricated what kind of Jesuses out of what biblical knowledge combined with idiosyncratic theologies as affected by their perceptions of the current events of their times, including their particular hopes, fears, resentments and uncertainties. The primary hypothesis of this study is that the hymnists under consideration depicted in their hymns the Jesuses that fit best with their situation in life at the time the texts were composed, and, furthermore, that the hymnists' internal visions of Jesus were almost entirely subjective and should not be taken as representing any actual historical figure, much less the one or ones hidden in the texts of the New Testament and proclaimed in the propositions of the creeds.

Note: Works cited in the following section will not always have page numbers. In several cases, the author had to piece together bits of sometimes otherwise undocumented information about the hymnist or the circumstances of his or her life. Complete references to all cited titles appear in the Bibliography.

Safe in the Arms of Jesus

Fanny J. Crosby, 1868

Safe in the arms of Jesus, safe on His gentle breast,
There by His love o'er shadowed, sweetly my soul shall rest.
Hark! 'tis the voice of angels, borne in a song to me.
Over the field of glory, over the jasper sea.

Safe in the arms of Jesus, safe from corroding care.
Safe from the world's temptations, sin cannot harm me there.
Free from the blight of sorrow, free from my doubts and fears;
Only a few more trials, only a few more tears.

Jesus, my heart's dear Refuge, Jesus has died for me;
Firm on the Rock of Ages, ever my trust shall be.
Here let me wait with patience, wait till the night is o'er;
Wait till I see the morning break on the golden shore.[17]

Fanny J. Crosby (1820–1915) was born blind. She married Alexander Van Alstyne, also blind, at the age of thirty-seven, having been his friend for more than fifteen years. A daughter was born to that marriage in 1858, dying in infancy from what was probably typhus. Fanny outlived Van Alstyne by almost seventeen years. In the intervening time she composed over eight thousand hymn texts, many of which became perennial favorites in evangelical churches, and many of them are sung in such churches to this day. Crosby was born in New York and died in Connecticut, but her hymnody spanned a continent. She is considered the most prolific hymn writer in the history of Christianity, though that datum cannot be proven. She was forty-five by the time the War Between the States broke out and lived seven months into the beginning of the Great War in Europe. James Monroe was President of the United States when she was born; Woodrow Wilson was in the third year of his first term when she died. Crosby's life spanned the Victorian era and all of the Edwardian years. She was ninety-three when the Archduke of Bosnia was assassinated in June of 1914. She lived through the great cholera epidemic of 1849 in New York, the battles of Fort Sumter, Antietam, and Gettysburg; William Tecumseh Sherman's march through Georgia; Lincoln's assassination; the completion the transcontinental railroad; the assassination of James Garfield; the Spanish American War; and the Gilded Age.

Newspapers at the time of the ante-bellum cholera epidemic quoted ministers of all stripes opining that the widespread sickness was God exacting retribution for sin. Crosby, a frequent attendant upon the sermons of Henry Ward Beecher and great supporter of the Union, must have been aware of this passage from Lincoln's Second Inaugural Address:

> Neither party expected for the war, the magnitude, or the duration, which it has already attained. Neither anticipated that the cause of the conflict might cease with, or even before, the conflict itself should cease. Each looked for an easier triumph, and a result less fundamental and astounding. Both read the same Bible, and pray to the same God; and each invokes His aid against the other. It may seem strange that any men should dare to ask a just God's assistance in wringing their bread from the sweat of other men's faces; but let us judge not that we be not judged. The prayers of both could not be answered; that of neither has been answered fully. The Almighty has his own purposes. "Woe unto the world because of offences! for it must needs be that offences come; but woe to that man by whom the offence cometh!" If we shall suppose that American Slavery is one of those offences which, in the providence of God, must needs come, but which, having continued through His appointed time, He now wills to remove, and that He gives to both North and South, this terrible war, as the woe due to those by whom the offence came, shall we discern therein any departure from those divine attributes which the believers in a Living God always ascribe to Him? Fondly do we hope—fervently do we pray—that this mighty scourge of war may speedily pass

away. Yet, if God wills that it continue, until all the wealth piled by the bond-man's two hundred and fifty years of unrequited toil shall be sunk, and until every drop of blood drawn with the lash, shall be paid by another drawn with the sword, as was said three thousand years ago, so still it must be said "the judgments of the Lord, are true and righteous altogether."

It is not clear how any of that rhetoric affected the composition of her hymn texts, but the tenor of those times surely must have. She could not have been unaware of Walt Whitman's lament for Abraham Lincoln, "When lilacs last in the dooryard bloom'd."[18] Lincoln's death in 1865 came seven years after her only child's death. In the interim more than a half million American soldiers on both sides of the Mason-Dixon line had become corpses.

Safe in the arms of Jesus, safe on His gentle breast,
There by His love o'er shadowed, sweetly my soul shall rest.

Crosby's imagined Jesus was clearly a personification of the deity in which she evidently believed, but closer by far to her and those she knew had suffered and died than that deity as such—so close, in fact, that one's personal essence (soul) could be cradled in His arms. The biblical images that come immediately to mind are the pastoral ones of Psalm 23: "The Lord is my shepherd. . . . He leadeth me besides the still waters. . . . Yea, though I walk through the valley of the shadow of death, I will fear no evil; for thou art with me," along with the words attributed to Jesus by the author of John, "I am the good shepherd" (10:11, 14), and the following text from Isaiah 40, which, when sung to the aria from G. F. Handel's *Messiah*, can go far towards making a believer out of the most brittle of cynics: "He shall feed his flock like a shepherd: he shall gather the lambs in his arm, and carry them in his bosom, and shall gently lead those that are with young."

Something like that must surely have been awakened in Crosby's imagination as she wrote the line, "safe in the arms of Jesus." But it's a long haul thence from the combative Jesus depicted by the New Testament evangelists as confronting his detractors and attempting to put them in their place, or the Jesus upending the tables of the currency exchangers and the stools of the pigeon sellers in the Temple courtyard. The Crosby image is closer to that of John 20:14–18, the encounter depicted between Mary of Magdala and the resurrected Jesus in graveyard.

In the Garden

C. Austin Miles, 1912

I come to the garden alone,
While the dew is still on the roses;
And the voice I hear, falling on my ear,
The Son of God discloses.
And He walks with me,
And He talks with me,
And He tells me I am His own;
And the joy we share as we tarry there,
None other has ever known.

C. Austin Miles (1868–1946), a pharmacist-turned-hymn-writer seems to have seized upon the John 20 image in his 1912 hymn *In the Garden*, for which he also composed the score.[19] As noted in John 20:1, Mary Magdalene comes alone to the tomb on an unspecified errand.

Miles' own account suggests that he had been commissioned to write a hymn by a publisher for whom he later worked after he had put away his mortar and pestle. Miles, an amateur photographer, was sitting in his darkroom waiting for some prints to develop and he took up his Bible only to read the John 20 passage. Out of whatever was going on in his life, Miles said he had a three-dimensional vision of the event depicted in that passage. *In the Garden* became one of the most loved hymns of the twentieth century—and no wonder, as people wearied by grief over the death of loved ones could more easily grasp and be grasped by the sentimental longing visible in the text and audible in Miles' melody. Again, it is a picture of a very accessible Jesus that Miles's text paints, one that, an admirer of his wrote, has "the timeless power to tame grief" and "eases pain for all who sing it or hear it sung."

The text, however, is a clear case of eisegesis, that is, writing into a text what is not there. The exchange John depicts between Mary and a resurrected Christ is more attenuated than Miles' text suggests. Jesus asks Mary why she is crying and whom she is seeking. Not recognizing him and thinking he is the gardener (cemetery sexton) she merely asks where the corpse is so she may take it away. Jesus then speaks her name, causing her to exclaim "Rabbouni," or "My great one, my teacher." She is forbidden to touch him and is given instructions about what to tell the disciples. No walking, little talking, nothing about Mary being "His own," and little tarrying. In fact, the text conveys a sense of hurry and urgency. Also, if Mary was enraptured in a joy "none other has ever known," it is not evident in the text. John merely and rather flatly says she went to the disciples and told them she had "seen the Lord" and conveyed the things he had said to her. There is no indication that they paid any attention to her whatsoever.

It would be interesting to know what was going on in Miles' life at the time he composed the hymn. The year 1912 included the near-assassination of Theodore Roosevelt, the sinking of the Titanic, the death of Clara Barton, the second largest volcanic eruption in history (Novarupta in Alaska), the massive explosion of a meteorite over Holbrook, Arizona, and the discovery in Antarctica of the frozen corpses of explorer Robert Scott and his men on the Ross Ice Shelf near the South Pole—all chronicled in lurid newspaper headlines. It was the epic disaster of the Titanic's sinking and the enormous loss of life that settled over the American imagination for months after the event.

Sermons referencing the event were heard from pulpits all over the Western World. Perhaps the most remarked upon—especially in later years and in light of the 1917 Bolshevik Revolution—was that of the Swiss pastor and theologian Karl Barth, who boldly declared that the Titanic disaster was God's judgment on what he called the "crime of capitalism," in which the few vie with each other at the expense of the many for the sake of gain.[20] Thus Barth saw the Titanic as a piece of a larger picture at which both rich and poor were compelled to look and see themselves as both perpetrators and victims. Not as well focused or as articulate as Barth's analysis, sermons of other ministers kept firmly fixed the aural and visual images of people singing *Nearer My God to Thee* as the decks' slant grew steeper.

Surely Christians who had the resurrection in their theological portfolios would seek some reassurance that the black depths of an icy ocean would not be the last word. Quite naturally, one supposes, they took up such sentiments as expressed by Miles' text *In the Garden*. Miles may have appreciated the encounter of the living with the dead and their intimate communication ("Mary!") depicted in that Johannine passage as the perfect antidote to the haunting sight of drowning people, their dream ship sinking beneath the waves forever. So it was that a dawn meeting with a resurrected savior in a garden of bedewed roses depicted by a pharmacist whilst plying the techniques of his hobby became for millions of people a beguiling picture of a Jesus who cares.

In the Garden remains one of the most popular church hymns enduring into the twenty-first century and is among the most requested for Christian funerals and memorial services. CDs of its various performances are in the audio library of virtually every funeral home powered by electricity. At the same time the hymn is the bane of most professional church musicians, who despise its saccharine lyrics and overly chromatic score. Except in venues where their judgment is not appealable, *In the Garden* is heard over and over again.[21]

Nothing but the Blood

Robert Lowry, 1876

What can wash away my sin?
Nothing but the blood of Jesus;
What can make me whole again?
Nothing but the blood of Jesus.
O! precious is the flow
That makes me white as snow;
No other fount I know;
Nothing but the blood of Jesus.
Nothing can for sin atone,
Nothing but the blood of Jesus;
Naught of good that I have done,
Nothing but the blood of Jesus.[22]

Robert Lowry (1826–99) was an academician, a professor of literature, in fact. He studied theology at what was then known as the University of Lewisburg (Penn.), now Bucknell College, returned to teach literature there, and eventually became its chancellor. He was also a Baptist minister. He gave much time and energy to the composition of hymn texts, some five hundred, in fact. Though he was best known and is best remembered as a hymnist, he longed to be considered a top-flight "gospel preacher."

Nothing but the Blood was written eleven years after the ending of the War Between the States, when American society remained bitter about the conflict and was still mourning its dead. Newspaper and magazine articles continued to report emerging details about the great battles, especially of Gettysburg, notable for its gore. Lewisburg is almost due north of Gettysburg by eighty-five or so miles. Lowry could not have taught and preached in that part of Pennsylvania without mentioning the great battle that took place there. The theme of blood so associated with Civil War imagery surfaced in the text of his best-known hymn. He appended to the published copy a quotation from Heb 9:22: "Without the shedding of blood there is no for-giveness of sins" (NRSV).

The American Baptists had split into north-south over the is-sue of slavery as early as 1845. Lowry would have known many of his clergy colleagues in the South and, as a minister himself, understood the terrible burden on his brother pastors in comfort-ing the families of Confederate soldiers who had died in com-bat of the 1861–65 war. A good many of the dead were almost surely Baptists themselves. Their shed blood must somehow be redeemed or seen as redeemed. How undoubtedly better than to see that blood in light of the blood Jesus is said to have shed on the cross? According to the Gospel of John, he had been crucified in the company of two others—Luke said they were "criminals." The clear implication was that Jesus was understood to be part of the criminal element as well. Yet, as later theology would work it out, the blood he shed as an executed criminal would have a salutary effect for believers. And that, in turn, may help twenty-first-century Christians appreciate, if not understand, the frequent allusion to blood in the kind of hymns we are consider-ing in this study.

If Lincoln's dabbling in theology ("If we shall suppose that American Slavery is one of those offences which, in the provi-dence of God, must needs come, but which, having continued through His appointed time, He now wills to remove, and that He gives to both North and South, this terrible war, as the woe due to those by whom the offence came . . .") was meant to sug-gest that combatants on both sides were paying the price for their political leaders' decisions, it could be construed by such hymnists as Lowry that their blood could be redemptive in the way the Bible considered Jesus to be redemptive. *Nothing but the Blood*, then, marks down Jesus as a victim, however willing, and his fleshly sacrifice as essential to the redemption of sinners as the blood of the war dead was to the healing of the nation.

Fanny Crosby got into the act as well with the refrain of her hymn *I Am Thine, O Lord*:

> Draw me nearer, nearer blessed Lord,
> To the cross where Thou hast died.

> Draw me nearer, nearer, nearer blessed Lord
> To thy precious bleeding side.

Blood is no longer unclean as Hebraic tradition says it is.[23]

By 1876, the year in which Lowry composed *Nothing but the Blood*, the depredations of Reconstruction were more and more evident. The massacre of Native American tribes in the westward push of the nation's commercial interests and the Wild-Wild-West, Jesse-James environment so vividly captured in twentieth-century Hollywood oaters featured more blood, innocent and otherwise. In fact, Jesse James and his gang of robbers were at the height of their criminal careers in 1876. James himself would be dead in just six years, shot in the back by a bounty hunter.

While we are considering Robert Lowry, it would be well to set out the text of one of his hymns that is sung to this day on Easter Sunday in many an evangelical church—*Up from the Grave He Arose* (1874).

> Low in the grave he lay, Jesus my savior,
> waiting the coming day, Jesus my Lord:
> Up from the grave he arose,
> with a mighty triumph o'er his foes;
> he arose a victor from the dark domain,
> and he lives forever with his saints to reign.
> He arose! He arose! Hallelujah, Christ arose!
> Vainly they watch his bed, Jesus my Savior,
> vainly they seal the dead, Jesus my Lord!
> Up from the grave . . .
> Death cannot keep its prey, Jesus my Savior;
> He tore the bars away, Jesus my Lord:
> Up from the grave . . .[24]

The text is built, of course, on no objective data whatsoever. It is an assertion worthy of the docetic heresy,[25] as "waiting the coming day" suggests that Jesus only seemed to be dead when buried. The words "Up from the grave he arose, / with a mighty triumph o'er his foes; / he arose a victor from the dark domain . . ." resemble a stage direction for a drama. Of what *foes* does Lowry write? And was he envisioning the grave or tomb as part of the underworld? And was his text meant metaphorically? "Vainly," he wrote, "they watch his bed," and "vainly they seal the dead." Did he mean that it was all an act, that the outcome was known beforehand?

And what of the "mighty triumph o'er his foes"? Lowry might have had in mind some of the more lurid passages of the Revelation of St. John the Divine as he turned his pen to that phrase. Fundamentally, in Lowry's eyes, those who are depicted as lovingly taking Jesus' corpse from the site of his execution to the temporary tomb and left it there until the women would come and finish the job were simpletons because "Death cannot keep its prey." There's another term that turns a grisly execution into a hunting expedition, where the *prey* is finally snatched from the jaws of the trap or extracts itself.

No offense meant to Lowry, but in a world that operates on a rational basis, honoring the profound insights of Copernicus, Galileo, Newton, Darwin and Einstein, Easter can have nothing to do with a dead body rising to life and eventually ascending into heaven, let alone it having first been born of a virgin. All of that is the worst kind of falsehood—worst because it leads people to look beyond this here and this now to some there and then for which no data exists. Heaven and individual immortality are inventions of people frightened into selfishness, who insist upon living in denial of the plain facts of life—and of death.

Old Isaiah had it right: "The grass withers; the flower fades. . . . Surely the people are grass" (40:7; NRSV).

The truth embedded in the Isaiah strophe represents the kind of Easter Christians who know their New Testament can claim for themselves and share with any and all is set forth in a much-quoted and much misunderstood verse from the Gospel of John: "And you will know the truth, and the truth will make you free" (8:32; NRSV). That truth is that all life in the biosphere is transient.

The Greek word commonly translated in English as "truth" means "the reality lying at the base of appearance," in practice "unveiling" or "disclosure." What is disclosed, and how does it set free? An Auschwitz survivor told me once that it was the self-realization that however unfree his Nazi jailers had made him, he remained free to experience freedom inwardly and to envision it actually. He told me that in the morning when he was roused by the din set up by the capos he sometimes found himself smiling because he had before him a day to live. Maybe then he'd have another and even another. That was his truth.

African Americans know something about freedom and about its opposite. Their parents and grandparents and great-grandparents knew what Martin Luther King Jr. meant when, in bringing his "I Have a Dream" speech to a conclusion, he echoed the refrain of an old spiritual: "Free at last! Free at last! Thank God almighty we're free at last"—that is, if not quite yet from the physical lash of slavery at least from its psychic burden.

King knew even as late as fifty years ago at the time of his epoch-making 1963 speech that many African Americans were not free at last or free at all. They lived still, many of them, in the bondage of poverty, subject to the dictates of a white society and a whites-only grasp on power. Yet King knew that he and they were free in the same way the survivor of Auschwitz knew he was free, even as he wore the striped garb of a prisoner over the emaciated flesh of what was left of him. Both the preacher and the prisoner experienced and envisioned their freedom—the latter by keeping on despite the horrors of dying and death on every hand, the former by affirming it when it was yet in vulnerable infancy.

Such truth means that life is not properly measured in significance by length, but by depth. If the grass withers—which it most certainly does—and if the people surely are grass—which we most certainly are, the key to freedom is to embrace that knowledge and then, like the survivor and Dr. King, to find each day an amazing gift, however grim may be its immediate prospects.

The Cleansing Wave

Phoebe W. Palmer, 1867

Yet more blood. Phoebe Palmer (1807–??) was the mother in a mother-daughter team of hymnists, both named Phoebe. The elder Phoebe W. Palmer was the lyricist; the younger Phoebe Palmer Knapp was the score composer. Mrs. Palmer was born and lived in New York City, where she was swept up in the holiness revival movement of Methodism. She led a prayer meeting in which, it is said, bishops and theologians were frequent participants. Known as the mother of the holiness movement, she wrote several books, and her articles appeared in religious journals.

Two years after the end of the War Between the States, she wrote her most popular hymn text:

> O, now I see the crimson wave,
> The fountain deep and wide;
> Jesus, my Lord, mighty to save,
> Points to his wounded side.
> The cleansing stream I see, I see!
> I plunge, and Oh, it cleanseth me;
> Oh, praise the Lord, it cleanseth me,
> It cleanseth me, yes cleanseth me.[26]

Where did Palmer get such an idea? Below are a number of texts that deal with the belief in blood's (Jesus') salvific efficacy:

> Jesus said to them, "I tell you the truth, unless you eat the flesh of the Son of Man and drink his blood, you have no life in you." (John 6:53)

> But now in Christ Jesus you who once were far away have been brought close through the blood of Christ. (Eph 2:13)

> Therefore, brothers, since we have confidence to enter the Most Holy Place by the blood of Jesus. (Heb 10:19)

49

To Jesus the mediator of a new covenant, and to the sprinkled blood that speaks a better word than the blood of Abel. (Heb 12:24)

And so Jesus also suffered outside the city gate to make the people holy through his own blood. (Heb 13:12)

This is the one who came by water and blood—Jesus Christ. He did not come by water only, but by water and blood. And it is the Spirit who bears the witness, because the Spirit is the truth. (1 John 5:6)

But if we walk in light, as he is in the light, we have fellowship with one another, and the blood of Jesus, his Son, purifies us from all sin. (1 John 1:7)

For this is My blood of the new covenant, which is shed for many for the remission of sins. (Matt 26:28)

But now in Christ Jesus you who once were far away have been made near by the blood of Christ. (Eph 2:13)

For the life of the flesh is in the blood. . . . For it is the blood that makes atonement for the self. (Lev 17:11)

He has delivered us from the power of darkness and transported us into the kingdom of the Son of His love, in whom we have redemption through His blood, the forgiveness of sins. (Col 1:13)

And they overcame him by the Lamb's blood and by the word of their testimony, and they did not love their lives to the death. (Rev 12:11)

And they sang a new song, saying: You are worthy to take the scroll, and to open its seals; for You were slain, and have redeemed us to God by Your blood out of every tribe and tongue and people and nation. (Rev 5:9–10)

How much more shall the blood of Christ, who through the eternal Spirit offered Himself without splotch. The blood will be a sign for you on the houses where you are; and when I see the blood, I will pass over you. No destructive plague will touch you when I strike Egypt. (Exod 12:13)

What a Friend We Have in Jesus

Joseph Scriven, 1857

Joseph Scriven (1819–86) grew up in the Church of Ireland and was a graduate of Trinity College, Dublin, but eventually embraced the ways and beliefs of the Plymouth Brethren. His first love and fiancée, a young woman from Banbridge, was thrown from her horse into the River Bann and drowned as he stood watching from the other side. In his grief he decided to leave Ireland for Canada, where he lived in Port Hope, Ontario, from 1842 until his death. There he met another woman, Eliza Roche, to whom he became engaged. They were to be married in 1854, but Miss Roche contracted a respiratory disease to which she succumbed three years later in 1857. Scriven, now twice widowered, turned inward to his religious belief and ethic.

To comfort his mother grieving for him back in Ireland, he composed in that same year a poem entitled *Pray without Ceasing*, based, one supposes, on that very admonition of St. Paul found at 1 Thess 5:17. The imperative can be understood as commanding a life of attentiveness to the presence of God, which presence is acknowledged by theists through the forming of thoughts and words to express such thoughts, as it were, to a listening human ear. Hence some of the best known and loved verse in the English-speaking world depicting Jesus no longer as a bloodied victim, nor yet as teacher of morals, but as a faithful friend and intermediary on whom one can and should rely when dealing with human sorrow.

> What a friend we have in Jesus,
> All our sins and grief to bear!
> What a privilege to carry
> Everything to God in prayer.
> O what peace we often forfeit,

O what needless pain we bear,
All because we do not carry
Everything to God in prayer.

Have we trials and temptations?
Is there trouble anywhere?
We should never be discouraged;
Take it to the Lord in prayer!
Can we find a friend so faithful,
Who will all our sorrows bear?
Jesus knows our every weakness;
Take it to the Lord in prayer.

Are we weak and heavy laden,
Cumbered with a load of care?
Precious Savior, still our refuge;
Take it to the Lord in prayer.
Do your friends despise, forsake you?
Take it to the Lord in prayer!
In His arms He'll take and shield you;
You will find a solace there.[27]

Who would make that verse his own will encounter what the systematic theologian would call role confusion. It is a question for theists, of course, but is the purpose of prayer to connect the friend in whose arms one can be taken and shielded, or to the transcendent *theos*? Scriven's text, composed in grief, was probably not intended as a theological but rather a pastoral statement. The grieving could care less on whom they might lean if they have the slightest hope of finding that person, power, or personality.

Jesus as friend and as the intermediary between the vivid, all-too-real sorrows of human life and the imagined author of life itself comes as a comforting and helpful image to the believer. It does not seem as if Scriven was thinking or writing in metaphor. That Jesus about whom he had learned as a catechumen and whom he had preached was a friend to whom he felt he could reach out. He wanted to convey that thought to his grieving mother as he felt so deeply his own grief for not one but two removed: those dear ones whom he had loved and lost.

The record shows that Scriven continued his quiet and unprepossessing ministry to the poor of southeastern Canada, literally giving up the coat as well as the cloak to those who had need of them. In so doing, Scriven became the same kind of friend of whom his famous verse had spoken. Many a preacher has accounted for Jesus in large and larger terms, often reaching for the "King of kings and Lord of lords" figure. Scriven was content to call him a friend. This humanist would say of such an idea that Scriven *was* what he himself sought through the medium of prayer. He was the friend, and the tributes said to have been spoken upon his death suggest that was so.[28]

Tell It to Jesus

Jeremiah Rankin, 1888

Continuing on the theme of Jesus as friend and confessor, we turn to a hymn composed by a Protestant minister, Jeremiah Eames Rankin (1828–1903), who served Methodist, Presbyterian, and Congregational churches from Vermont in the north to Washington, DC, in the south. He taught homiletics and practical theology at Howard College (later Howard University) where he was president from 1890–1903. An abolitionist and advocate of temperance, he was a favorite preacher of members of Congress during the time that he led the First Congregational Church in the nation's capital. Besides *Tell It to Jesus*, Rankin's other perhaps more famous hymn text is *God Be with You 'til We Meet Again*. He fancied himself a poet as well as a preacher and ecclesiastical figure — and a political philosopher as well. His best-known sermon ("The Divinity of the Ballot") was widely published throughout the country. Its theme is not hard to discern. Rankin believed that an American's fundamental duty was to be informed and to cast the vote on the basis of that information. He saw it as part of one's divine calling.

It may seem odd that Rankin, an academician and activist, would have taken the time to write such a simple text as *Tell It to Jesus*. Yet he did teach pastoral theology to would-be clerics and, for all of his visibility and involvement, apparently did not neglect the finer points of human sentiment.[29]

> Are you weary, are you heavy-hearted? Tell it to Jesus,
> Tell it to Jesus; Are you grieving over joys departed?
> Tell it to Jesus alone.
> Tell it to Jesus, Tell it to Jesus,
> He is a friend that's well-known;
> You've no other such a friend or brother,
> Tell it to Jesus alone.

Do the tears flow down your cheeks unbidden? . . .
Have you sins that to men's eyes are hidden? . . .
Do you fear the gath'-ring clouds of sorrow? . . .
Are you anxious what shall be tomorrow? . . .
Are you troubled at the tho't of dying? . . .
For Christ's coming Kingdom are you sighing? . . .[30]

The questions posed in that text are rhetorical. Rankin assumed that someone somewhere was heavy-hearted, weeping, anxious, and troubled. He might have known that from his years as a parish minister. As his early pastorates were served during the War Between the States, it stands to reason that he officiated at many a funeral for slain Union soldiers. The occasion for such services could not have helped but cause "grieving over joys departed" in his parishioners, along with unbidden tears flowed freely in gathering clouds of sorrow "at the tho't of dying." Almost every American—Yankee and rebel alike—after April 1865 must have been "anxious what shall be tomorrow."

Since Rankin did not publish the text of *Tell It to Jesus* until 1888, he may have been working from memory. By 1888 the beginnings of the Gilded Age were in sight; the transcontinental railroad had been in business for a dozen years. The movers and shakers of Reconstruction were turning their attention from punishing former plantation owners to the subjugation of the "freed slaves" and instituting a reign of terror that would not abate until the modern Civil Rights movement.

For Christian believers, the sentiments of Rankin's hymn text provided a comforting image, because a lot of people had plenty to tell to Jesus, that "friend that's well-known." How well-known was the figure of Jesus among American Protestants in 1888 and after? Jesus was seen as the über-pastor, the Protestant confessor, the all-around Good Guy on whose warm shoulder one could lay his head and confide his sorrow, his fear, and his dread. To such a friend in need, the Protestant Jesus, loosed from the categories of systematic theology, was a friend indeed.

I Need Thee Ev'ry Hour

Annie Sherwood Hawks, 1872

I need thee ev'ry hour, Most gracious Lord,

No tender voice like Thine Can peace afford.

I need thee, O, I need Thee; Ev'ry hour I need Thee!

O bless me now, my Savior, I come to Thee.

I need Thee ev'ry hour, Stay Thou near by:

Temptations lose their pow'r When Thou art nigh . . .

I need thee ev'ry hour, In joy or pain;

Come quickly and abide, Or life is vain . . .

I need Thee ev'ry hour, Most Holy One;

Oh, make me Thine indeed, Thou blessed Son.

Annie Sherwood Hawks (1835–1918) was yet another friend in need. Not only did she need Jesus "ev'ry hour," in another Hawks hymn the tables were turned: "He needs me every hour." Hawks wrote more than four hundred hymn texts, but *I Need Thee Ev'ry Hour* is the only one that has survived in continued use. She was not a "little house on the prairie" woman — far from it. She was born in Hoosick, New York, immediately west of the Vermont-New York border but lived in Brooklyn for most of her life, where she was married, kept house for her husband, and had three children with him. The Hawks family joined a Baptist church. She was active in the Sunday school. She had dabbled in poetry since girlhood and began to write religious verse with the encouragement of her pastor, Dr. Robert Lowry who, as it turned out, composed the score for *I Need Thee Ev'ry Hour* and, in fact, for many of her hymn texts. It was first published in a Sunday school hymnal in 1873.[31]

The undocumented story of the hymn is that whilst engaged in her housework on a certain June morning in 1872, the words to the text came to her. Housework, even for urban wives of that era, could not have been much of a picnic, as the common appliances that would come along in a later era were not part of the average household. If Mrs. Hawks did not have a laundress, she would have washed her family's clothing and household linens with a tub and washboard and dried them on an outside line whilst the dust and dirt of city life fell upon it. Brooms and feather dusters were the means of household dirt removal—and not particularly satisfactory at that. What food refrigeration existed was provided by ice boxes, that is, metal boxes shod with hardwood into which blocks of ice were lifted by the proverbial ice man. Unless Mrs. Hawks had a maid of all work or a cook, she was required to go out on a daily basis, excepting Sunday, to obtain food for meals.

In that way, Mrs. Hawks was typical of middle-class women of her era, separated from the husband's work life, her life circumscribed by the drudge of daily chores, the rearing of children with all that entailed, largely removed from any position of leadership and therefore without a voice in public affairs. Faithfulness, at least on her part, is the assumption we make about the Hawks' marriage, but the intimacy of the text *I Need Thee Ev'ry Hour* certainly makes one think. Perhaps Mrs. Hawks was far ahead of her time in coping with the isolation of domestic life almost a century before the women's liberation movement of the 1960s and 1970s. She apparently found an outlet for what may have been her frustration and discontent by transferring to her inner image of Jesus, the friend, her longing to be heard, attended to, hovered over (dare I say "pampered") by the Savior of her imagination. She wants to be made "Thine indeed." She will "come to Thee." A possible clue to the depth of her feeling is this line: "Temptations lose their pow'r When Thou art nigh." What temptations did a Brooklyn housewife in 1872 entertain? She said they had "pow'r," but they vanish in the Savior's—or the husband's—presence. And what sins could she imagined having committed beyond, perhaps, envy of someone with a less dreary life than hers or of another woman whose husband may have been more attentive than her own? Hard to know.

Withal, one can infer from the text that Mrs. Hawks saw Jesus as immediately available to her through the medium of prayer, for that is what the hymn is, directly addressed to Jesus, though he is never named, only referred to as "Most gracious Lord," "Most Holy One," and "Savior." However she imagined him, she somehow knew he had "a tender voice" that could "peace afford." One wonders if Mr. Hawks looked at or remarked upon the hymn text and what he might have felt in doing so? Maybe the attentive pastor, Dr. Lowry, was the savior-substitute. That happens to male clergy and their women parishioners far more often than acknowledged or discussed publicly. Lowry ended up composing many a score for Annie Hawks' hymns. They had, therefore, at some level a co-equal status—something she probably did not have otherwise and probably could not have had, given the expectations laid upon housewives in the mid-nineteenth century.

Softly and Tenderly

Will Lamartine Thompson, 1880

Softly and tenderly Jesus is calling,
Calling for you and for me.
See, on the portals He's waiting and watching.
Watching for you and for me.
Come home, come home, Ye who are weary, come home,
Earnestly, tenderly Jesus is calling,
Calling, O sinner, come home.

Why should we tarry when Jesus is pleading,
Pleading for you and for me?
Why should we linger and heed not his mercies,
Mercies for you and for me . . .
Time is now fleeting, the moments are passing,
Passing for you and for me;
Shadows are gathering, death beds are coming,
Coming for you and for me . . .
O for the wonderful love He has promised,
Promised for you and for me;
Tho' we have sinn'd He has mercy and pardon.
Pardon for you and for me . . .

Will Lamartine Thompson (1847–1907) was born in Smith's Ferry, Pennsylvania, but grew up in East Liverpool, Ohio, to a mercantile family and a father who went into state politics. He spent several terms at Mt. Union College in Alliance, Ohio, before attending the New England Conservatory of Music in Boston, and later studied music in Leipzig, that beehive of musical composition and performance and seat of the J. S. Bach revival that had been sparked by Felix Mendelssohn. Anybody who was anybody in the music world of the era stopped for a time in Leipzig. There stood the Thomas Kirche, famed for its one-time choir master—Johann Sebastian Bach himself—as the site of many a performance of a Bach cantata, sometimes with the ink still not quite dry on the score. It seems that Thompson, who composed the tune of his most noted hymn text (*Softly and Tenderly*), did not pick up much of the Leipzig spirit. You cannot imagine the lead soprano in the *Kirchenchor* in the Thomas Kirche singing either the text or the tune of this hymn. It does not compute. No more so in Thompson's day would you have been likely to hear *Es ist nichts Gesundes an meinem Leibe* (BWV 25) anywhere in East Liverpool, Ohio, except possibly in a Lutheran church, and that by a choir composed of off-duty firemen, the town baker with a dusting of flour still on his coat, a furloughed railroad conductor, and a woman piano teacher who fancied herself a diva.

Thompson must have known that, his Leipzig days notwithstanding, and began to put his musical talents, such as they might have been, to the composition of the kind of songs such as would later be heard on radio and gouged into phonograph records—a mix of patriotic songs, which were popular in the post-bellum days, and such ballads as *My Home on the Old Ohio*.[32] His work did not at first sell well until he self-published some of his songs. The ode to the Ohio River and another called *Gathering Shells from the Sea* became hits, as we would now say, and made him wealthy. He went into business selling sheet music and instruments from East Liverpool and a branch in Chicago.

Whence, then, the hymns? Given the many Sunday school hymnals being published in the second half of the nineteenth century and the appetite for easy-to-sing, easy-to-remember texts and tunes, Thompson—with evident faith and piety—plunged into hymn writing. The story (undocumented) goes that, resenting the greats of the day making appearances in large cities in pre-vaudeville days to perform to crowds, he loaded an upright grand into a wagon and drove across the countryside playing and singing in country churches. It was likely in just such venues that such hymns as his *Softly and Tenderly* struck home to those (especially women) who did not necessarily hear any voice that was soft and tender, where life was tough and subject to weather abnormalities, the invasion of insects, monster snowstorms, dried-up wells, and rapacious bankers who would foreclose on farm and house if a monthly payment on a loan was missed by a day.

A voice calling in such a manner, "Come home, come home, ye who are weary, come home," would surely have resonated with people trying to eke out life under such circumstances— "home" meaning whence they came or "home" meaning a promised heaven. The hymn gained popularity when it was published in Thompson's *Sparkling Gems No. 1 & No. 2* and even greater attention when sung by actress Geraldine Page in the 1985 movie *A Trip to Bountiful*.

Jesus, Savior, Pilot Me

Edward Hopper, 1871

Jesus, Savior, pilot me
Over life's tempestuous sea;
Unknown waves before me roll.
Hiding rock, and treach'rous shoal;
Chart and compass come from Thee;
Jesus, Savior, pilot me.

As a mother stills her child,
Thou canst hush the ocean wild;
Boist'rous waves obey Thy will
When Thou say'st to them, "Be still;"
Wondrous Sov'reign of the sea . . .

When at last I near the shore,
And the fearful breakers roar
'Twixt me and the peaceful rest,
Then, while leaning on Thy breast,
May I hear Thee say to me
"Fear not, I will pilot thee."

Edward Hopper (1816–88) was born, lived, and worked in New York City for all of his life, save eleven years in Greenville and Sag Harbor (Long Island), New York. He was a graduate of New York University and of the Union Theological Seminary, also of New York. He was for eighteen years the minister of the Presbyterian Church of the Sea and Land in lower Manhattan that had been founded as a mission for mariners, who then were numerous around the southern tip of that borough. The edifice was built in 1819 when Hopper was an infant. The hymn's first appearance was anonymous entry in the *Sailor's Magazine* in the same year as it was written.[33] It was spotted early on by the New

York composer, conductor and music store owner John E. Gould, who set the still-anonymous text to music.[34]

Sometime later the secretary of the Seaman's Friend Society, Samuel Hall of Newark, N.J., asked Hopper, a natural source, for a hymn text to celebrate an anniversary of the society. Hopper sent him the text of *Jesus, Savior, Pilot Me*. The hymn may first have been sung by the congregation of the Broadway Tabernacle on May 10, 1880.[35] Over the years and decades, it has been reprinted in dozens of Sunday school and gospel hymnals including a mid-twentieth century Congregation Church hymnal,[36] a late twentieth century United Methodist hymnal[37] and a 1988 Free Will Baptist hymn collection.[38] It became known that Hopper was its author when the text was read aloud—perhaps by Hopper himself or at the very least in his presence—at a seamen's society meeting.

While the hymn text was probably written based on the stories with which seamen had regaled Hopper and with their nautical labors in mind, those who sang it down the years began to take it as a metaphor for life with its "tempestuous seas," "unknown waves," and "treacherous shoals." The farther along one gets in the hymn the more metaphorical it becomes, with the sea pilot becoming a mother comforting her child and an allusion to Matt 8:23–27 (Jesus calming the waves amid his disciples' fear). Finally, in the third stanza Hopper turned to what may have been on his mind all along, the coming of death. There Jesus, the pilot, is to replace the mother stilling her child, holding the dying one and leading him into a peaceful death.

The hymn originally had six stanzas. Those that appear in most contemporary hymnals are the first, the fifth and the sixth. Others speak of "the Apostles' fragile bark" struggling "with the billows dark," a more direct reference to the Matthew 8 text; and of a reminder that, when things are going just so very well, it is wise to remember just then the potential need of a pilot:

> Though the sea be smooth and bright,
> Sparkling with the stars at night.
> And my ship's path be ablaze

With the light of halcyon days,
Still I know my need of Thee;
Jesus, Savior, pilot me.

Hopper, friend of seafarers, must have known what nautical pilots do. They do not guide ships over "tempestuous seas" or "oceans wild" nor yet over "boist'rous wave." Rather, they assist ships' masters in negotiating the entrance to harbors that may have a "hiding rock" or two, or a "treach'rous shoal." But the pilot guides; he does not command and does not order maneuvers. Hopper's text does not ask Jesus to command or order. It asks Jesus to pilot, suggesting that the master of whatever ship will listen to suggestions and information, or he will not, finally having his own self to blame if he ignores the pilot's guidance. Perhaps he read Erasmus on the subject of free will, to the effect that one may spurn that which will save him.

Jesus Loves Even Me

Philip P. Bliss, ca. 1870

I am so glad that our Father in heaven
Tells of His love in the book He has giv'n.
Wonderful things in the Bible I see.
This is the dearest that Jesus loves me.
I am so glad that Jesus loves me, Jesus loves me, Jesus loves me.
I am so glad that Jesus loves me, Jesus loves even me.

Tho' I forget Him and wander away,
Still He doth love me wherever I stray.
Back to His dear loving arms I would flee,
When I remember that Jesus loves me . . .
Oh, if there's only one song I can sing,
When in His beauty I see the great King.
This shall my song in eternity be.
Oh what a wonder that Jesus loves me . . .

Philip P. Bliss (1838–76) had the distinction of being born in a lowly log cabin somewhere in the vicinity of Rome, Pennsylvania, about twelve miles south of the New York State border in northeastern Pennsylvania. His father, Isaac, was a serious practitioner of Methodism, and apparently inculcated in his son the discipline of daily prayer and hymn singing. Young Isaac warmed to this latter exercise and was indulged in elementary music. The family removed to Kinsman, Ohio, just five miles west of the Pennsylvania border, when Bliss was six years old, and returned to the Keystone State three years later to settle there in Tioga County in the north central region—much moving about for family in those years before the general availability of dependable rail transportation.

Bliss was without the benefit of any kind of regular formal education. At a young age he found work in lumber camps and timber mills and out of season tried to attend rural schools to learn the basic subjects then taught in them. His mother earlier had taught him the Bible, whatever that might have meant in the 1840s and 1850s—probably the order of the books of the Bible with what we would call today a fundamentalist take. It is difficult at this remove to understand how in 1855 at the age of seventeen he was credentialed as a teacher, but by 1856 he was ensconced as a principal of a school in Hartsville, New York, in Steuben County about fifteen miles north of the Pennsylvania border, not all that far from where he was born.

Bliss' talents as a singer led him to take up work as an itinerant teacher of music. He married in 1859—one Lucy Young who had been raised in the Presbyterian Church, and as a result embraced that tradition. He tried writing a few songs, but none, insofar as is known, was ever issued by a publisher. He was drafted into the Union infantry in the last months of the War Between the States but never served in combat. Meanwhile, Bliss and Lucy had removed to Chicago, where he gained modest fame as a singer and instructor in music. In the late 1860s Bliss and Dwight L. Moody found each other, with the former coming under the influence of the latter. Bliss had composed by then a number of hymns that were popular in evangelical circles, but he decided to give most of his time and effort to actual preaching.

His life and that of Lucy's came to tragic end in 1876 when a train in which they were traveling near Ashtabula, Ohio, fell off a trestle, dragging its passenger cars with it into an inferno in which they both perished. Their remains were never identified. They left behind two sons under the age of five.[39]

Bliss composed his hymn *Jesus Loves Even Me* while he was associated with a Congregational Church in Chicago and at the height of his powers. He apparently thought in the rhyming style of period hymnody and so from his pen flowed both the text and the music of this hymn at hand. The text represents the intertwined themes of the bibliocentric religion of mid-to-late nineteenth-century piety, stressing an ever-present Jesus who was believed to love "even me"—this latter point being, perhaps, the outworking of the kind of guilt that can be, often was, and sometimes is yet instilled in children and young people by fundamentalist teachers and clergy.

By mid-nineteenth-century standards, Bliss led a charmed life — until the Ashtabula train wreck. Why would not the Jesus of his imagination with "his dear loving arms" have embraced him for his advocacy of the gospel by the written and preached word and the music that went with them?

Sweet By and By

Sanford F. Bennett, 1868

There's a land that is fairer than day;
And by faith we can see it afar;
For the Father waits over the way
To prepare us a dwelling place there.
In the sweet by and by
We shall meet on that beautiful shore.
In the sweet by and by,
We shall meet on that beautiful shore.

We shall sing on that beautiful shore
The melodious songs of the blest,
And our spirits shall sorrow no more,
Not a sigh for the blessing of rest . . .
To our bountiful Father above
We will offer our tribute of praise,
For the glorious gifts of His love
And the blessings that hallow our days . . .

Sanford F. Bennett (1836–98) was a man of many talents and evidently of much ambition. He was born in Eden, New York, now a part of suburban Buffalo. His family moved to Wisconsin and at some point he attended the Waukegan Academy (Wisconsin) and later the University of Michigan. He received a medical degree from Rush Medical College in Chicago in 1874. He served in the 40th Wisconsin Volunteers during the War Between the States, but his unit was activated only for three months.[40] A writer of some talent, he published essays and poems in various Midwestern newspapers. After a stint as a school principal, he became a pharmacist (probably before his medical training) and operated what at the time was still called an apothecary in Elkhorn, Wisconsin, where most sources say he wrote his most famous and for practical purposes only surviving hymn still in use, *Sweet By and By*. The story, largely undocumented, is that Bennett was busy one day filling prescriptions when Joseph Webster, a local musician and friend, walked in with a budget of unexpressed disappointment. Bennett asked what as the matter, and Webster said it was nothing that would not pass "by and by."

On the strength of that brief exchange it is said that Bennett, the prolific writer and poet, sat down forthwith and scrawled out what must be one of the most popular hymns of the era and since. Nothing known about Bennett suggests that he was particularly devout, but he could not have helped being exposed to popular piety. His facility with prose and poetry may have fitted him well for the writing of what he may have thought was just one more piece of verse. The public educator, pharmacist, doctor and Civil War veteran may have lived long enough to understand what an impact his three-stanza hymn text, set to a tune by the man whose mild complaint inspired it, would have in the world of Protestant evangelical circles.

Take the Name of Jesus with You

Lydia Odell Baxter, 1870

> Take the Name of Jesus with you,
> Child of sorrow and of woe,
> It will joy and comfort give you;
> Take it then, where'er you go.
> Precious Name, O how sweet!
> Hope of earth and joy of heav'n.
> Precious Name, O how sweet!
> Hope of earth and joy of heav'n.
> Take the Name of Jesus ever,
> As a shield from every snare;
> If temptations round you gather,
> Breathe that holy Name in prayer . . .
> At the Name of Jesus bowing,
> Falling prostrate at His feet,
> King of kings in heaven we'll crown Him,
> When our journey is complete . . .

Lydia Odell Baxter (1809–74) was born in Petersburg, New York, about twenty miles east of Troy near the Vermont border. She grew up there and in her youth experienced a conversion together with her sister after hearing the preaching of Eben Tucker, an itinerant evangelist. She later married an army colonel, John Baxter, and soon moved with him to New York City. There she was busy with Sunday schools and other evangelical work. She became ill in her middle age with an undiagnosed ailment that left her largely bedridden. Notwithstanding, she conducted evangelical work from her sickbed, encouraging others to do what she could not do herself. She wrote poetry, some of which was published in 1855 as *Gems by the Wayside*. She composed hymn texts, the best known of which are *Take the Name of Jesus with You* and *The Gate Ajar*. This latter hymn became popular in the evangelistic crusades of Dwight L. Moody held in England in the year or so before Baxter's death at sixty-four.[41]

Baxter was apparently convinced that the "name" of Jesus was portable—not that she herself was much able to go places in her invalid condition. But it could be portable for others in the same way as rosaries are to devout Catholics and a pocket New Testament is to Bible-believers. Was she aware that the biblical term "name" when in its texts it is applied to the deity or to the Christ figure means "nature," as in "the nature or disposition of God or of Jesus?" To take the perceived nature of the Bible's God "with you" would be to take the power of mercy and justice "where'er you go." That's probably not what Baxter meant; rather, hers seemed to be the idea that the spoken name was a kind of lifeline which one could grasp when thrown into the deep waters "of sorrow and of woe."

Such faith was not uncommon among nineteenth-century evangelical Christians not yet having been given the opportunity of considering the findings of the historical-critical work with the biblical text. However, when that opportunity came it was a bridge too far for most of them to cross. They had become comfortable in their beliefs in the efficacy of such things as "the Name of Jesus" and were not anxious to be parted from them. The theology of Lydia Odell Baxter and many of her religious compatriots eventually would be challenged by the observations of Charles Darwin and the exponents of higher criticism in the universities and seminaries during the last half of the nineteenth century. It does not seem that Baxter was much aware of what was to come.

Jesus Saves

Priscilla J. Owens, 1882

We have heard the joyful sound: Jesus saves! Jesus saves!
Spread the tidings all around: Jesus saves! Jesus saves!
Bear the news to ev'ry land,
Climb the steeps and cross the waves;
Onward! 'tis our Lord's command, Jesus saves! Jesus saves.

Waft it on the rolling tide; Jesus saves! Jesus saves!
Tell to sinners far and wide: Jesus saves! Jesus saves!
Sing ye islands of the sea; Echo back, ye ocean caves;
Earth shall keep her jubilee: Jesus saves! Jesus saves!

Sing above the battle strife: Jesus saves! Jesus saves!
By His death and endless life: Jesus saves! Jesus saves!
Sing it brightly through the gloom,
When the heart for mercy craves;
Sing in triumph o'er the tomb: Jesus saves! Jesus saves!

Give the winds a mighty voice: Jesus saves! Jesus saves!
Let the nations now rejoice: Jesus saves! Jesus saves!
Shout salvation full and free, Highest hills and deepest caves;
This our song of victory: Jesus saves! Jesus saves!

Priscilla J. Owens (1829–1907) was a lifelong resident of Baltimore, Maryland, where she taught in public schools and was active in the Union Square Methodist Episcopal Church Sunday school. She wrote essays and poetry samples that appeared in *The Christian Standard* and Methodist publications.[42] She seemed to have been representative of devout Protestant women of the age, quite totally devoted to church and Sunday school work and to the education of children.

Her hymn *Jesus Saves* is far better known than she. It is heard on radio and television evangelistic programs, often sung, and that with full voice, to organ and piano accompaniment. It employs over and over again the phrase "Jesus saves," almost as a mantra. It is a celebration of a surety held dear by those who believed and believe as Ms. Owens evidently believed, namely, that a person—no matter how good, no matter how much good he or she does—is condemned to eternal death instead of being raised bodily when the general resurrection occurs in end times, unless he or she believes that "Jesus saves."

If evangelical hymnody has a creed, this hymn is it. The phrase "Jesus saves" is ubiquitous on car bumpers, church bulletin boards, and tee shirts. It is found in unlikely places scrawled on restroom walls, sides of buildings, overpasses and railway cars. What that simple declarative sentence may mean to anyone responsible for its appearance is unknown. If a person's motive to display it is consonant with the certitude of Owens' hymn, then it is pure proclamation of what can most charitably be called a surmise based on nothing other than biblical passages that say as much.

It is a missionary hymn written by someone who seldom, if ever, left the city of her birth. Some of its expressions call to mind Reginald Heber's 1819 composition *From Greenland's Icy Mountains*. The verb *waft* appears in both hymns. The idea of carrying the message across oceans and to other lands is forcefully expressed in both. Heber has the mandate as "Waft, waft, ye winds, His story, and you, ye waters, roll." Owens's text says: "Waft it on the rolling tide . . . tell to sinners far and wide . . . bear the news to ev'ry land. . . . Onward! 'tis the Lord's command."

Owens spares us Heber's imperialistic language, namely, "They call us to deliver their land from error's chain. . . . The heathen in his blindness bows down to wood and stone." Owens' was probably focusing on the unconverted white folk of Baltimore, some of whom she may have known, rather than the Indian masses of Calcutta to which Heber was posted as a bishop in 1823. He had written his missionary hymn four years earlier and may have repented of its tone, because he died on the afternoon of the day he preached a sermon critical of the caste system to thousands in a torrid outdoor setting. The worst Owens says about those she considered ignorant of the proposition that "Jesus saves" was that they were "sinners far and wide."

An interesting note is that the text was adapted to follow the meter of the chorus of "Vive le Roi" in the 1836 opera *Les Huguenots* by Giacomo Meyerbeer. Billy Graham meets Italian opera.

Jesus Loves Me

Anna B. Warner, 1860

Jesus loves me! this I know,
For the Bible tells me so;
Little ones to Him belong,
They are weak but he is strong.
Yes, Jesus loves me, Yes, Jesus loves me,
Yes, Jesus loves me, the Bible tells me so.

Jesus loves me! He who died,
Heaven's gate to open wide;
He will wash away my sin,
Let His little child come in . . .
Jesus take this heart of mine,
Make it pure and wholly Thine;
Thou hast bled and died for me,
I will henceforth live for Thee . . .
Jesus loves me! He will stay
Close beside me all the way;
He's prepared a home for me,
And someday His face I'll see . . .

Anna B. Warner (1820–1915) and her sister Susan Warner, although born in wealth, lived in penury as a result of the 1837 panic that ruined their father, Henry. They wrote stories and poems for a living. They are unknown now except to book collectors and scholars of the period. The sisters collaborated on a novel called *Say and Seal* in which a young boy is dying whilst his Sunday school teacher holds him in his arms singing a song: "Jesus loves me, this I know . . ." It was the second most popular piece of fiction of the period, the first being Harriet Beecher Stowe's *Uncle Tom's Cabin*.[43] *Say and Seal* was soon eclipsed by the hymn *Jesus Loves Me*, perhaps the best-known Protestant Sunday school hymn in the history of the movement. The tune for it is widely credited to the composition of William B. Bradbury (1816–68), who, it is said, read the Warner sister's novel and spotted the "Jesus love me" line, then set it immediately to the well-known if somewhat simplistic tune to which it has since been sung.

Bradbury is credited with the scores of such hymns as *He Leadeth Me* (text by Joseph Gilmore), *Just As I Am* (text by Charlotte Elliott), *Sweet Hour of Prayer* (text attributed to a William Walford), and *Savior, Like A Shepherd Lead Us* (text attributed to Dorothy A. Thrupp).

It happens that upon their removal from a handsome New York City residence after their father's financial collapse, the sisters moved to an old home on Constitution Island in the Hudson River adjacent to the US Military Academy, where they conducted bible study classes for the cadets—before the days of the American Civil Liberties Union. One can see the Warner home today on the grounds of West Point.

It is not unreasonable to think that their Bible instruction for the cadets, many of whom would serve in the War Between the States, included mention or even singing of *Jesus Loves Me*, with the line "Jesus loves me! He who died, Heaven's gate to open wide; He will wash away my sin, Let his little child come in," which could have succored many a young lieutenant or captain on the battle fields of that bloody war—maybe even as they lay dying.

Jesus Loves Me is the very first Sunday school song the author can remember hearing and singing. He heard his mother sing it to him, and later to his younger sisters as a lullaby. As sing-songy the score, as elementary the text, Anna Warner's hymn has said it all for millions of children for more than 150 years. It is a pity that the text rests on wispy and out-of-context biblical snippets that do not take into account the deeper and more conflicted themes of the literature. Withal, the hymn stands as a monument to the strange institution known as "the Sunday school," which plenty of red-blooded American boys of my generation attempted to avoid like the plague. I was taunted for actually enjoying Sunday school.

Let Jesus Come into Your Heart

Lelia Naylor Morris, 1898

If you are tired of the load of your sin,
Let Jesus come into your heart;
If you desire a new life to begin,
Let Jesus come into your heart.
Just now, your doubtings give o'er;
Just reject Him no more;
Just now, throw open the door;
Let Jesus come into your heart.

If 'tis for purity now that you sigh,
Let Jesus come into your heart;
Fountains for cleansing are flowing nearby,
Let Jesus come into your heart . . .
If there's a tempest your voice cannot still,
Let Jesus come into your heart;
If there's a void this world ne'er can fill,
Let Jesus come into your heart . . .
If you would join the glad songs of the blest,
Let Jesus come into your heart;
If you would enter the mansions of rest,
Let Jesus come into your heart . . .

Lelia Naylor Morris was born in Pennsville, Ohio, in 1862 and lived her entire life in the state. She married Charles H. Morris at the age of nineteen in 1881. The Morrises made their home in McConnelsville, Ohio. She was active in the Trinity Methodist Episcopal Church there, where today a state historical marker honors her long ministry of music in the congregation where, it is said, she wrote more than one thousand gospel songs. Born while her father was in the Union army, her life encompassed most of the War Between the States, the post-bellum push into the Plains and Far West, thanks to the building of the transcontinental railroad. It is not known what she thought about Reconstruction and its treatment of African Americans. Her life was apparently a-political and totally devoted to the pursuit of her faith, the writing of hymns (both text and tune) and serving her Methodist church as its organist for many years. The Methodist camp meeting Holiness movement was a venue for her work, as well. It was at once such camp meeting in Mountain Lake Park in Maryland that she wrote or was inspired to write her best-known hymn *Let Jesus Come into Your Heart*. In later years as her sight failed, her son constructed a large 28-foot wide blackboard with a magnified staff enabling her to continue to compose until total blindness overtook her late in life. In the end, she and her husband lived with their daughter in Auburn, Ohio where Mrs. Morris died on July 23, 1929 at age of sixty-seven.[44]

The Holiness movement of the mid-to-late nineteenth century would have a thematic descendant in the evangelical enthusiasm of the late twentieth and early twenty-first century, as theologically conservative factions began to dominate in mainline denominations, especially the United Methodist Church. The Holiness movement that Morris embraced was such an enthusiasm. It may have begun when lawyer-turned-evangelist Charles Finney began to preach in 1824 associated with the Female Missionary Society. He turned Jonathon Edward's soteriology on its head in deciding that salvation was to be a work performed by human beings on their own behalf. They would have to attain unto holiness on their own.[45]

Methodism in particular was fired by the Holiness movement as its *Discipline*[46] was amended by dress-code regulations directed mostly at women, perhaps echoing an admonition mistakenly attributed to St. Paul at 1 Tim 2:9–10 ("Women should dress themselves modestly and decently in suitable clothing . . ."; NRSV). Begun in the ante-bellum years when some Methodist adherents saw slavery as immoral, it continued once the war was over in a demand that worldliness be stamped out.[47] As part of the pursuit of holiness, one was required to seek purity in life and to lay on Jesus the burden of one's sin—the word "sin" covering a multitude of moral errors. Much as Roman Catholics are instructed to make acts of contrition and to confess their sins to a priest in order to receive absolution, so such holiness-minded Methodists were instructed to take their sins to Jesus in prayer, to invite Jesus into their hearts where he might become aware of the hidden nature of what Morris called "the load of your sin" should they "desire a new life to begin." Such a new life would banish "a tempest your voice cannot still" and having Jesus enter your heart would take the place of "a void this world never can fill."

Holiness Methodists, according to Morris' hymnic understanding, had to choose between Jesus in their hearts and the world. The idea was "Just now, your doubtings give o'er; Just now, reject him no more," and finally to "Just now, throw open the door," a possible allusion to Rev 3:20: "Behold, I stand at the door. And knock: if any man hear my voice, and open the door, I will come into him" (KJV).

Onward, Christian Soldiers

Sabine Baring-Gould, 1865

Onward, Christian soldiers,
Marching as to war,
With the cross of Jesus
Going on before:
Christ the royal Master
Leads against the foe;
Forward into battle,
See his banners go.
Onward Christian soldiers,
Marching as to war,
With the cross of Jesus going on before.
Like a mighty army
Moves the Church of God;
Brothers, we are treading
Where the saints have trod;
We are not divided,
All one body we,
One in hope and doctrine,
One in charity . . .
Crowns and thrones may perish,
Kingdoms rise and wane,
But the Church of Jesus
Constant will remain;
Gates of hell can never
'Gainst that Church prevail;
We have Christ's own promise,
And that cannot fail . . .
Onward, then, ye people,
Join our happy throng,
Blend with us your voices
In the triumph song;

Glory, laud and honor
Unto Christ the King;
This through countless ages
Men and angels sing . . .

Sabine Baring-Gould (1834–1924) was a scholar of no mean accomplishment, having published eighty-five volumes over half a century, including theological works and those treating of mythology, biography, travel and the art of preaching.[48] Consequently Baring-Gould should not be judged by the apparent militant nature of this hymn, it having been hurriedly composed, after all, as a Sunday school procession. Nor should it be thought a trifle because Arthur S. Sullivan, he of the comic operetta fame, furnished its tune. The hymn is of a muscular sort, unlike some others analyzed in these pages, not in the least passive or retiring, not depicting Jesus as a personal friend and life's companion. Also unrevealed in the hymn's text is Baring-Gould's Wesley-like outreach to the poor and unlettered. In his first parish assignment in the coal mining region of Yorkshire, he saw the need of basic education for both youths and older men who worked in the collieries by day, and so founded at his own expense a night-school in his spartan apartment in the village of Horbury Bridge.

Baring-Gould was not your average English vicar. He was educated in both Germany and France and took his degree from Clare College, Cambridge, becoming a scholar in several fields. He came to write the text to *Onward, Christian Soldiers* out of a perceived need to make enjoyable a Whitmonday procession of his Sunday school pupils to a parish in a neighboring village for a joint service. It is said that he dashed off the text in a matter of a quarter of an hour[49] and was astonished that what he considered mere, convenient verse became a wildly popular standard favorite not only in the Church of England but throughout Protestantism, in whose churches it is still sung in 2013.[50]

Baring-Gould could not have been unaware of the Crimean War that England had concluded in April 1856 after the ghastly defeat of the Queen's Light Brigade in the Battle of Balaclava on October 25, 1854. That defeat, in which England suffered 278 casualties, with more than half that number slaughtered, an unknown number of prisoners of war taken by Russian troops, and the loss of 355 horses.[51] The war concerned, among other things, the place of the declining Ottoman empire's sultanate and the protection of Christian holy sites in Palestine. The Crimean conflict was the first to be reported by electric telegraph and so was more immediate to the readers of British newspapers and was all the talk of towns large and small. One can almost see in Baring-Gould's mind images of the medieval crusades with their armies moving forward under the banners of cross and crown—and not just "as" to war, but to war itself. Journeyman scholar and historian that he was, Baring-Gould might also have thought of "the cross of Jesus going on before" as the vision Constantine the Great confessed to seeing, leading him to embrace Christianity.

Lactantius tells of Constantine the night before what turned out to be the decisive battle (that with Maxentius) resulting in his winning the leadership of the Western empire. The future emperor had a dream on the eve of his subjugation of Maxentius in which he saw a *chi* (**X**) and a *rho* (P), being the initial letters in the name "Christ" (Χριστος). He caused what is now known as the Chi/Rho to be monogrammed on to his armor and that of his soldiers. Constantine credited his battlefield conversion for his success, believing that the cross of Jesus had, in fact, gone on before him.[52]

Baring-Gould also could not have been unaware of the instantly famous verse from England's poet laureate, Alfred Lord Tennyson, *The Charge of the Light Brigade*:

> Half a league, half a league,
> Half a league onward,
> All in the valley of Death
> Rode the six hundred . . .
> When can their glory fade?
> O the wild charge they made!

All the world wonder'd.
Honor the charge they made!
Honor the Light Brigade,
Noble six hundred.[53]

Baring-Gould's hymn was an answer to Tennyson's verse. The church of Jesus Christ would survive any martyrdom to which its faithful soldiers in Christ would ever suffer:

Crowns and thrones may perish,
Kingdoms rise and wane,
But the Church of Jesus
Constant will remain;
Gates of hell can never
'Gainst that Church prevail;
We have Christ's own promise,
And that cannot fail . . .

Stand Up, Stand Up for Jesus

George Duffield, Jr., 1858

> Stand up, stand up for Jesus, ye soldiers of the cross;
> Lift high His royal banner, it must not suffer loss.
> From vict'ry unto vict'ry His army shall He lead,
> Till ev'ry foe is vanquished, and Christ is Lord indeed.

Out of the same kind of aggressive evangelical determination as the Baring-Gould text implies, Duffield's hymn, of which only the first of six stanzas appear above (more than sufficient to get the direction of the whole), while written more than a century and a half ago, is sung today in many a church as a kind of summons to evangelize the unchurched to go battle with evil. Subsequent stanzas speak of putting "the foe to rout," letting "courage rise with danger" and proving to all "that death itself is gain." It is a hymn that means business.

Duffield (1818–88) was a graduate of Yale and the Union Theological Seminary of New York. A Presbyterian minister, he served churches in Brooklyn, NY; Bloomfield, NJ; Philadelphia, PA; Adrian, MI; Galesburg, IL; and Saginaw, Ann Arbor, and Lansing, MI, where at one time he was a regent of the University of Michigan.

It was during his eleven-year Philadelphia pastorate that Duffield became friends with an Episcopal colleague, the Rev. Dudley Tyng, rector of Church of the Epiphany. Tyng was very much the evangelist but also a firebrand preacher for the cause of abolition. It is said that on his deathbed Tyng, when asked by devotees for last words, said, "Let us all stand for Jesus."[54] In turn, Duffield preached a sermon of tribute the very next Sunday in the city's Temple Presbyterian Church, which he closed with a six-stanza poem: *Stand Up, Stand Up for Jesus*. The hymn endures to this day and is especially prized by evangelists staging revivals.

Duffield's Jesus is an army general leading fearless conscripts against the unbelieving and unbelievers. Whatever foe deserves vanquishing will fall before this mighty army. The military motif continues with reference to putting on armor—no doubt an allusion to Eph 6:13–17 that calls for putting on *the whole armor of God*, the fastening on of *the belt of truth* and the donning of *the breastplate of righteousness, the shield of faith* and *the helmet of righteousness*. The writer of that passage—most New Testament scholarship doubts that it is directly of Pauline provenance—seems to have been thinking metaphorically. It seems clear that Duffield went a step further to say that those who would stand up for Jesus would take anything that helped them stand, to keep them standing and to march on to victory against whatever stood in their way.

Have Thine Own Way, Lord
Adelaide A. Pollard, 1902

Have thine own way, Lord! Have thine own way!
Thou art the potter, I am the clay.
Mold me and make me after thy will,
While I am waiting, yielded and still.

Have thine own way, Lord! Have thine own way!
Search me and try me, Savior today!
Wash me just now, Lord, wash me just now,
As in thy presence humbly I bow.

Have thine own way, Lord! Have thine own way!
Wounded and weary, help me, I pray!
Power, all power, surely is thine!
Touch me and heal me, Savior divine!

Have thine own way, Lord! Have thine own way!
Hold o'er my being, absolute sway.
Fill with thy Spirit till all shall see
Christ only, always, living in me.

Adelaide Addison Pollard (1862–1934) was born Sarah in Bloomfield, Iowa. In early adulthood she changed her first name to Adelaide.[55] She died seventy-two years later in New York City. She was stricken in a railroad station and soon thereafter died. She had been about to travel to New Jersey for a speaking engagement or two.[56] Some years before, she had studied at the Denmark Academy in Iowa and later in Valparaiso, Indiana, also in Boston at the city's School of Oratory. She had hoped to become a missionary to Africa, but did not get to that continent until shortly before the First World War began in 1914. In middle and late adulthood she was associated with religious groups that were considered by most to be out of the mainstream. She seldom visited her Iowa family, who were strict Calvinists. She was considered to be a mystic by many who knew her. She never married. Apparently she wrote extensively in the literature of hymnody, but the one that survives and is still sung in the early twenty-first century is *Have Thine Own Way, Lord.*

The hymn draws scripturally on Jer 18:3–6 for the image of potter-and-clay: "Then the word of the Lord came to me: Can I now do with you, O house of Israel, just as this potter has done? says the Lord. Just like the clay in the potter's hand, so are you in my hand, O house of Israel" (NRSV). "Mold me and make me after thy will," Pollard wrote. The reference to being washed may call to mind Ps 51:7b: "Wash me, and I shall be whiter than snow" (NRSV). Even though both the Jeremiah and Psalms texts refer to the Hebrew deity (in Jeremiah, *Lord*; in the Psalm, *God*) and Exod 19:10–11 describes the washing of garments in preparation for the coming of the Lord on Mt. Sinai, Pollard may have been thinking also of Ps 139:23 as she wrote her second stanza: "Search me, O God, and know my heart; test (try) me and know my thoughts" (NRSV). If her hymn is any indication, Pollard's philosophy of religion posited the deity of the Bible as absolute and the free will of the human being non-existent except for the capacity to invite complete surrender to God's "absolute sway" (stanza 4). The aim seemed to be that she would be transformed from within to become a Christ-figure for all who looked upon her to see— "Fill with thy Spirit till all shall see / Christ only, always, living in me." In that is a hint of the mysticism it is said that many of her acquaintances saw in her.

At times there is a flash of sexuality in the text, such as "Mold me and make me after thy will / while I am waiting, yielded and still"; and "Hold o'er my being absolute sway." This latter language calls to mind Luke 1:35, Gabriel explaining to Mary of Nazareth how she will become pregnant: "The holy spirit will come to lie over you . . ."—One wishes there was more to be known about Adelaide Pollard's life that would illuminate her supposed mysticism.

More about Jesus Would I Know

Eliza E. Hewitt, 1887

More about Jesus would I know,
More of His grace to others show;
More of His saving fullness see,
More of His love Who died for me.

More, more about Jesus,
More, more about Jesus;
More of His saving fullness see,
More of His love Who died for me . . .

More about Jesus let me learn,
More of His holy will discern;
Spirit of God, my teacher be,
Showing the things of Christ to me . . .

More about Jesus; in His Word,
Holding communion with my Lord;
Hearing His voice in every line,
Making each faithful saying mine . . .

More about Jesus; on His throne,
Riches in glory all His own;
More of His kingdom's sure increase;
More of His coming, Prince of Peace . . .

Eliza E. Hewitt (1851–1920) was a lifelong resident of Philadelphia, Pennsylvania, and was educated in its public schools, in which she eventually taught for a number of years. Her persona was that of the "old maid school teacher," who, when she wasn't teaching Monday through Friday, taught in Sunday schools. For many years she was superintendent of a Sabbath school at the Northern Home for Friendless Children. In subsequent years, she ran the young children's Sunday school at the Calvin

Presbyterian Church. Like many of her persuasion, she was wont to write poetry, most of it religious in nature, including gospel hymns. When a serious spinal injury took her to an invalid's bed, she kept on writing even as she read broadly in English literature, which broadened her appreciation of the language. She never married but gave her life to the education of children.[57]

The hymn under consideration, like many of its kind, focused on the persona of Jesus, that figure that tended to seem more accessible to Protestant believers in the nineteenth century. It was a time of sentimental, almost romantic piety. What was the "more" about? What did Hewitt as a student, albeit a lay one, want to know about Jesus beyond the stories in the gospels? That's all anybody has known since the first century CE. Supposing that the Jesus variously depicted in the gospels was a real person who lived in a real place and time, what more could be known?

Taking her hymn title seriously, one would assume that Hewitt was writing about acquiring a deeper understanding of the Jesus of the gospels, a more acute appreciation of his teaching and more inspiration to put it into practice, as in the ethical application: "More of His grace to others show." There the word *grace* would not necessarily carry its traditional theological meaning, but rather as pleasant countenance and behavior—the friendly and gentle Jesus that frequently shows up in Sunday school morality lessons. *More* is the key word. The nature of Hewitt's approach to Christianity, despite her static, bedridden years, was apparently dynamic, progressive, and lasting.

She wrote of the Spirit of God being her "teacher" and "Showing the things of Christ to me." What things would they be? The possible answer may be in the previous line: "More of His holy will discern." How would a rational, twenty-first century person discerns Jesus' will? He or she would take his ethical wisdom seriously, internalize it, and put it to work in turning the other cheek, walking the second mile, loving enemy as well as neighbor, giving up cloak and coat, forgiving the debtor, and treating others as one wishes to be treated.

The emphasis on learning and knowing more is that of a born educator, which Hewitt was. She was the valedictorian in the year of her graduation from Philadelphia's Girl's Normal School. Had she been aware of or attentive to the historical-critical approach to scripture, how much greater a contribution could she have made to the religious education of her charges? With no disrespect of her person and no disparagement of her contributions to the care and education of children, it might be said that Hewitt was the very model of the well-meaning Sunday school teacher, perhaps too anxious to introduce to her pupils a Jesus who never existed—a Jesus that would eventually be known by the insipid 1935 oil portrait by Warner Sallman called *Head of Christ*, which depicts a tanned, effeminate Anglo-Saxon male with long tawny, neatly brushed tresses, piously looking up as to the heavens. That Jesus, according to Nellie Talbot's 1900 Sunday school ditty wants us "for a sunbeam, / to shine for Him each day, / in ev'ry way try to please Him / at home, at school, at play."

Such a Jesus is what got drummed into the heads of generations of children in Protestant Sunday schools—a kind of benign scold who tsk-tsks from above at the miscreant and promises a spiritual lollipop if one is particularly good, speaks only when spoken to, does his or her chores without parental nagging and never has an evil thought—or at least never voices it. Little Bo Peep and Lord Fauntleroy come to mind. Hewitt is closer to profundity—but still leagues away—when she writes of "His saving fullness" and "of His love Who died for me." That "saving fullness," of course, was not a bloody death or a miraculous resuscitation but the gritty morality of passive resistance and truth-telling for which, if the various and sometimes contradictory gospel narratives can be believed, Jesus died.

In any event, anything about the Jesus of the gospels that one can teach or know or espouse with intellectual integrity is a good thing, regardless of theological or ecclesiological necessities.

I Heard the Savior Say

Elvina M. Hall, 1865

I heard the Savior say, "Thy strength indeed is small!
Child of weakness watch and pray,
Find in me thine all in all."
Jesus paid it all, All to Him I owe;
Sin had left a crimson stain—He washed it white as snow.
Lord, now indeed I find Thy power, and Thine alone
Can change the leper's spots.
And melt the heart of stone . . .
For nothing good have I
Whereby Thy grace to claim—
I'll wash my garments
In the blood of Calvary's Lamb . . .
And when before the throne I stand in Him complete,
"Jesus died my soul to save," My lips shall still repeat . . .

Elvina Mabel Hall (1820–89) was born in Alexandria, Virginia, and died in Ocean Grove, New Jersey. After the death of her first husband, Richard Hall, she married a Methodist minister named Thomas Myers and for the next forty years was a member of the Monument Street Methodist Church in Baltimore, Maryland.[58] Not a great deal more reliable information about her is available. It is, however, possible to infer a few things from the hymn text above.

Her verse, while typical of the somewhat teary sentimentality of the mid-to-late nineteenth-century hymn writers, is not doggerel. The second stanza is particularly striking for its meter and language: "Lord, now indeed I find Thy power, and Thine alone / can change the leper's spots / And melt the heart of stone." It scans very well. The idea of "changing" rather than "cleansing" the leper's spots is an inspired riff on the maxim to the effect that a leopard cannot change its spots. With that locution alone, Hall proved herself a poet of no mean ability. Melting the heart of stone is another arresting image.

Hanging it on what she "heard the Savior say," Hall captures the evangelical principle that the deity's strength is equal to human weakness so long as the human being finds that strength irresistible. Very Pauline. Very Augustinian. Very Lutheran. Hearing what the savior said seems to have been Hall's very subjective and poetic way of saying that she trusted the theology of grace as mediated through the Bible.

Hall bought the whole grace/redemption package by using the vivid image of her "garments" being washed "in the blood of Calvary's Lamb," by which washing she stands "in Him complete." The refrain of the hymn is more direct where blood is concerned. Drawing on the passage from Isa 1:18 ("Though your sins be as scarlet, they shall be white as snow"), Hall is not hesitant to say that it was Jesus' own blood literally shed on the cross that bought her and every other believer's way into salvation.

It is by rational standards an intellectually bankrupt theology but so well versified that one can see it for the poetry that it is. And if, as Archibald MacLeish is credited with saying, "A poem should not mean, but be," Hall's certainly is.

I'll Go Where You Want Me to Go

Mary D. Brown, 1871

It may not be on the mountain's height,
Or o'er the stormy sea,
It may not be at the battlefront
My Lord will have need of me.
But if by a still, small voice
He calls to paths I do not know,
I'll answer, dear Lord, with my hand in Thine,
I'll go where you want me to go.[59]

Mary D. Brown, for whom no birth or death date is available, apparently lived in Jewett City, Connecticut, in the last years of the nineteenth century. That may explain the connection with Charles E. Prior (see n. 59).[60] Where she lived in 1871, when she wrote *I'll Go Where You Want Me to Go*, is not clear. It is said that she gave her life to "working for Jesus," whatever she meant by that. Her hymn became far better known than she ever did, appearing in many a hymn collection well into the twenty-first century.

It is in its own way a missionary hymn written in a time when missionary societies were writ large in Protestant Christianity, and when it was believed among devout church members that it was a Christian duty to convert the unchurched to belief in the saving power of Jesus. What Brown seems to be saying in her one-stanza hymn is that whatever it takes to produce such conversions will be worth the giving of it. She named a "mountain's height," a "stormy sea," and a "battlefront" as venues in which she would be (or would want others to be) willing to go to spread the Word. In such places and under whatever circumstances, she evidently believed that she and others were needed, that God or Jesus could not effect the desired conversions apart from human

cooperation. To what degree she was schooled in biblical literature is not clear, but she could have been thinking of Paul's ratio-
nale for mission work (Rom 10:14–15a; NRSV): "How are they to
call on one in whom they have not believed? And how are they to
believe in one of whom they have never heard? And how are they
to hear without someone to proclaim him? And how are they to
proclaim him if they are not sent?"

High mountains, normally treacherous; stormy seas, likewise
dangerous; and battlefronts with carnage on all sides would be
daunting enough even to adventurous men of the immediate
ante-bellum years of the nineteenth century, and unthinkable for
most women of the time. Brown doesn't mention any particular
battlefield, but those of the War Between the States were still
fresh in the American mind. Those battlefields produced such
statistics as these 1) more than two percent of the nation's inhabit-
ants died as a result of the war and 2) half of all of them remained
unidentified or accounted for.[61] Surely Brown would have known
of that blood-curdling total of those soldiers, both Union and
Confederate, killed between 1861 and 1865: more than 620,000.
Brave, indeed, is one who will go to such a place at the inner
bidding of a deity or a deity's supposed son to seek conversions.

Prior's second and third stanzas suggest that mountains, seas,
and battlefields need not be the primary destinations of one
who will go wherever he or she is sent. He mentions speaking
inspired words to sinners or those in the path of sin who may
be in such places as "harvest fields so wide, / Where I may labor
thru life's short day / For Jesus the Crucified." Domestic as well
as foreign missionary initiatives, Prior seems to have conjectured,
are important and necessary.

In both Brown's and Prior's verse there is visible the big "I" of
nineteenth-century piety. It is the individual who is at the center
of things. It is an "I" religion—all about "me." Or perhaps both
Brown and Prior had in mind the words of the young Isaiah, who
depicted his own response to what he took as a divine calling:
"Here am I, send me" (6:8; NRSV).

Bringing in the Sheaves

Knowles Shaw, ca. 1872

Sowing in the morning, sowing seeds of kindness,
Sowing in the noontide and the dewy eve,
Waiting for the harvest and the time of reaping—
We shall come rejoicing, bringing in the sheaves.
Bringing in the sheaves, bringing in the sheaves,
We shall come rejoicing, bringing in the sheaves.

Sowing in the sunshine, sowing in the shadows,
Fearing neither clouds nor winter's chilly breeze;
By and by the harvest and the labor ended—
We shall come rejoicing, bringing in the sheaves . . .
Going forth with weeping, sowing for the Master,
Though the loss sustained our spirit often grieves;
When our weeping's over, He will bid us welcome—
We shall come rejoicing, bringing in the sheaves . . .

Knowles Shaw (1834–78) was never as well known in or after his lifetime as this hymn text that he wrote—the only one of his that appears to have survived. The author of this book conducted an unscientific experiment in word recognition by asking thirty-six people one at a time—typical Midwesterners, both Caucasian and African-Americans with a sprinkling of second and third generation Koreans and Chinese—if they recognized the name Knowles Shaw. Not a one of them, including two ministers and a choir director. I asked the same people to complete the sentence beginning with "Bringing in the _____." Of the thirty-six, twenty-nine immediately said "sheaves." Two said, "morning paper"; two said, "groceries"; two said, "mail"; and one said, "a salary," having ignored the definite article. The experiment contingently satisfied my somewhat shaky hypothesis to the effect that *Bringing in the Sheaves* may be one of the best-known gospel hymns in American church history.

If Shaw had died of old age instead of being one of a number of victims killed in a disastrous train wreck just outside of Dallas, Texas, on June 7, 1878, we would probably know even less about him than we do. We know that he was born in Butler County, Ohio, in 1834. When still an infant his parents moved to a rural area of Indiana where his father farmed and later ran a store. Shaw joined the church when he was twenty-one years old, taught school briefly before taking up the work of an evangelist, preaching wherever and whenever the opportunity presented itself. His preaching eventually led him to the offer of a pulpit in Chicago, but he resigned it to return to his evangelical itinerancy in Indiana. Such a mission took him hundreds of miles to Texas in June of 1878 where, after a successful mission in a Dallas church, he boarded a train to an engagement in McKinney, Texas, and died in the rail accident.[62]

Though it is nowhere mentioned in the slim record of Shaw's life, it stands to reason that living on his father's Indiana farm acquainted him with the planting and the harvesting of field crops, and the demanding work of a farmer. He would have known through experience that farming is a 24/7 operation "in the noontide and the dewy eve" requiring a good deal of patience in "waiting for the harvest and the time of reaping." Did he find the work of preaching as demanding and wearying as farming? Perhaps not, but he drew the analogy nonetheless. "Sowing in the sunshine, sowing in the shadows, / Fearing neither clouds nor winter's chilly breeze" would be a little like preaching in evangelistic settings, never knowing if you were connecting with an audience or congregation and if you had inspired a good number to come to the altar call. Traveling evangelists, like traveling salesmen, have to brace themselves for disappointment. But evidently both Shaw's farmer father and Shaw himself, the evangelist, had known the happiness that comes of success, namely, "By and by the harvest and the labor ended— / We shall come rejoicing, bringing in the sheaves."

One could safely assume that Shaw's biblical and theological acumen was not vast, but he knew enough to get end-times into his hymn with the allusion to what an English hymnist called "glad fruition, Faith to sight, and prayer to praise."[63] Shaw's vision of the eschaton was bright enough, but getting there was another thing: "Going forth with weeping, sowing for the Master, / Though the loss sustained our spirit often grieves." But he could envision a happy ending to the struggle—both in the crop field and in the pulpit "when our weeping's over, He will bid us welcome— / We shall come rejoicing, bringing in the sheaves."

I have heard this hymn sung in mainline Protestant churches by vested choirs led by four-manual pipe organs. I have heard it sung in the humblest country church with cattle lowing just outside open windows. I have heard it sung by my mother as she did the ironing. It was and is a perennial favorite among the devout and the sometimes devout, so familiar is it to the ear.

The Old Rugged Cross

George Bennard, 1913

On a hill faraway stood an old rugged cross,
The emblem of suffering and shame;
And I love that old cross where the dearest and best
For a world of lost sinners was slain.
So I'll cherish the old rugged cross,
'Til my trophies at last I lay down.
I will cling to the old rugged cross,
And exchange it some day for a crown.

O that old rugged cross, so despised by the world,
Has a wondrous attraction for me;
For the dear Lamb of God left His glory above
To bear it to dark Calvary . . .
In the old rugged cross, stained with blood so divine,
A wondrous beauty I see;
For 'twas on that old rugged cross Jesus suffered and died
To pardon and sanctify me
To the old rugged cross I will ever be true,
Its shame and reproach gladly bear;
Then He'll call me some day to my home faraway,
Where His glory forever I'll share . . .

George Bennard (1873–1958) was born the son of a coal miner in Youngstown, Ohio. The family moved to Iowa in the late 1870s, where Bennard experienced conversion at the hands of the Salvation Army and planned to be a gospel preacher. But when he was sixteen his father died, leaving Bennard to support his mother and his four sisters. He was unable to obtain the theological education that he craved and had to settle for the equivalent of "reading for orders" with the tutelage of older clergy. Eventually he moved the family to Illinois. Once married, he and his wife became leaders in the Salvation Army movement. Later, though, he left the Army and enlisted in the ranks of Methodism as an evangelist. Bennard is credited with composing as many as 325 gospel songs and hymns, but only one of them is sung today—and has been sung widely ever since he wrote it in 1913 while living in a rented room in Albion, Michigan, where he was the proprietor of a music concern. He lived most of his last years near Reed City, Michigan, where, on the west side of the old US 131 four and one-half miles north of town, there was put up in 1954 a large cross with a sign indicating the nearby home in which Bennard lived.[64] At 1101 E. Michigan Avenue in Albion stands a historical marker indicating that Bennard wrote *The Old Rugged Cross* on that site.

It may seem heresy to some, but it must be said that Bennard was a typical practitioner of me-centered Christianity. He used some form of the first-person eleven times in three stanzas, including five instances of *I*, two of *me*, two of *I'll* and two of *my*—as if what evangelical Christianity believes was a sacrificial act to extend eternal salvation somehow only applies to the particular individual among the ruck of "a world of lost sinners." Perversely, that may be the appeal of the hymn that is so often requested of high-minded church musicians at funerals, who think both the hymn's text and tune are execrable in every way.

The kind of sentiment Bennard expresses in the hymn has helped make the cross a universal symbol for struggle, defeat, and victory. One sees the cross everywhere, from the predictable spot atop a church steeple, to displays in some form or another at graves or on gravestones. The cross is fashioned for lapel pins, necklace pendants, earrings of both the pierced-ear and dangle types. It appears on bumper stickers and is associated with both protest against and advocacy of a lengthy spectrum of opinions and resentments. It appears on the front covers of bibles and prayer books. It adorns—or disfigures, depending on one's point of view—interior and exterior spaces of buildings. The cross has become more and more associated with in-your-face evangelical Christianity analogous, one hates to say, to the Nazi swastika, which itself is a malformed cross.

To my knowledge no one has ever scolded Bennard for making the cross into an idol or near-idol[65] as he confessed its "attraction" for him, that he would "cherish" it—at least until he laid down his "trophies."[66] It is to the cross, not his church or even his god, that Bennard says he "will ever be true," but at least "its shame and reproach gladly bear." By the time Bennard wrote the hymn, though, the cross had been "going on before" (as Baring-Gould put it) crusades and ideological conquests for centuries, no longer in any real way "The emblem of suffering and shame." But Bennard will embrace the cross and its religion, he says, as the *quid* in exchange *pro* the *quo* of everlasting life, as in, "Then He'll call me some day to my home faraway, / Where His glory forever I'll share."

Did Bennard and any of the people to whom he preached believe that the cross was a symbol of reproach and shame? Rather, one is entitled to assume that he and others saw it as a symbol of victory much as those who display the Confederate flag in the twenty-first century consider it a symbol of resentment and a warning of coming conflict rather than of the flat-out defeat it represented.[67]

What kind of religion is it that embraces, even symbolically, an individual's shame or suffering as a theological determinant? It is a psychologically unsound religion for one thing and lacking in the social sense of primitive Christianity in which the community was everything. The idea was to get beyond any of idea of shame because of one's commitment and suffering for the community, if necessary (cf. Mark 8:34–37). The cross was a weapon of intimidation and humiliation borrowed by the Romans from earlier Macedonian and Carthaginian cultures.[68] It was, in practice, an implement of executions. In our current culture, embracing an electric chair or gurney for lethal injections would be analogous to cherishing that old rugged cross.

And the idea that one can eventually turn in the embraced and bloody cross for a place in heaven cannot be considered sane, even in a metaphorical way. The god of people like George Bennard—and there were and are many, many of them—that could be conceived of as arranging for his son to be tortured to death through crucifixion for the sake of sparing believers the wages of sin, is not a god the rational person wants anything with which to do. It must be that Bennard had no idea of what crucifixion looked like and usually led to. The criminal did not bleed to death, perhaps shed no blood at all. But he could succumb to painful asphyxiation or the failure of the heart to pump blood to his head and upper extremities. If he survived or not, his leather fetters were eventually cut and his dying self or corpse left at the foot of the cross to be carrion for birds and wild dogs. In that sense the cross was a symbol of suffering and shame—but not the kind that a normal person would wish to cherish and embrace. However, it has been familiarly said by Christians that the blood of the martyrs is the seed of the church. Historians of Christianity point to such martyrdoms as that of Polycarp of Smyrna (ca. 155 CE), who went willingly to the stake because, essentially, he would not deny the deity of Jesus. The historians say his executors are to this day unknown by name, but him whom they burned alive became the patron saint of those determined to bear witness to what they believed to be true. You could put Mohandas Gandhi and Martin Luther King, Jr., in that category.

It should be noted that Bennard composed the tune to which *The Old Rugged Cross* is almost invariably sung. And as hymn tunes go, it is eminently singable as well as memorable. In fact, let the reader read the text without the accompanying tune and harmonization. If the reader doing so has never heard the hymn in its sung version, chances are that the text by itself would fall flat.

O Master, Let Me Walk with Thee

Washington Gladden, 1879

O Master, let me walk with thee
In lowly paths of service free,
Tell me thy secrets, help me bear
The strain of toil, the fret of care.

Help me the slow of heart to move
By some clear, winning word of love,
Teach me the wayward feet to stay,
And guide them in the homeward way.

Teach me thy patience; still with thee
In closer, dearer company,
In work that keeps faith sweet and strong,
In trust that triumphs over wrong.

In hope that sends a shining ray
Far down the future's broad'ning way,
In peace that only thou canst give,
With thee, O Master, let me live.

Washington Gladden (1836–1918) and his hymn are as far from Bennard and his hymn as Athens is from Borneo. Born Solomon Gladden, at age sixteen he dropped Solomon and was known thereafter as Washington. He began his adult life as a journalist and wrote during the rest of his life some forty books including *Applied Christianity* (1887), *Who Wrote the Bible* (1891), *Social Salvation* (1901) and *Christianity and Socialism* (1905). For a time, he wrote and edited for The New York Independent, and whilst there was active in exposing the corruption of Boss Tweed's Tammany Hall. An 1859 graduate of Williams College, Gladden became a minister of the Congregational Church in 1860 and

worked as a pastor for the next fifty-eight years in New York
State, Massachusetts, and, for more than a quarter of a century,
as pastor of the First Congregational Church of Columbus, Ohio.
Gladden was a leader of Congregationalism at the national level.
He served as the denomination's moderator from 1907 to 1909.
He resigned his Columbus pastorate in 1914 and died of a stroke
in 1918.

It was in his Ohio years that Gladden discovered, one might
say, the social gospel, or the application of the higher, historical-
critical method of understanding the Bible to the immediate
needs and concerns of people.[69] He had not been in Columbus
more than two years when the Hocking Valley coal strike broke
out in 1884. The mine owners, some of them, were prominent
members of Gladden's congregation and did not appreciate
his bible-based advocacy for the miners' welfare. The owners
crushed the miners' union in 1884 but lost out to them in a later
labor disruption, finally giving Gladden credit for his intervention with them on behalf of their workers.[70]

It seems that Gladden was not himself a socialist, nor yet a
capitalist, but he did make the connection between the ethical
wisdom attributed to Jesus of Nazareth in the synoptic gospels
and economic and social justice. He was, moreover, an early and
courageous advocate of a rational approach to such biblical documents as Genesis, saying that it was a waste of time to try to rec-
oncile its creation stories with the emerging sciences of biology
and geology. If Gladden did read Charles Darwin's *The Origin
of Species* that was published in the same year Gladden graduated from Williams, one wonders how it might have affected his
thinking, writing and preaching.

Gladden soon embraced the mission of what we would
now call anti-racism. He made the acquaintance of W. E. B.
Du Bois and spared no effort to disguise his own shock and
disgust of the treatment of African Americans during so-called
"Reconstruction" in the South.

His hymn *O Master, Let Me Walk with Thee* has been sung in
Protestant churches, less so in notably evangelical congregations,

for more than one hundred years and continues in usage, appearing in hymnals of the Episcopal Church USA, the Pilgrim Hymnal of Congregationalism, and the Free Will Baptist Hymn Book, to name but three of more than three dozen. The text reflects the straightforward declaration of the Epistle of James that faith apart from works is a dead letter (2:17). It is a gentle approach to the advocacy of the social gospel without the sometimes strident phraseology of later liberation theology. Gladden wrote of "lowly paths of service" in doing "work that keeps faith sweet and strong," knowing that those who in their work be required to "bear the strain of toil, the fret of care" would need encouragement and support in the doing of it.

Gladden was clearly optimistic about how the outworking of the social gospel in the practice of Christianity could create "hope that sends a shining ray / Far down the future's broad'ning way." That locution is an expression of a here-and-now humanism rather than of a then-and-there eschatology that has nothing to do with pressing and present need among human beings. That's what so distinguished Gladden's ministry and what made *O Master, Let Me Walk with Thee* a hymn that will be sung down the years by well-intentioned people trying to do good for no other reason than it is the right thing to be done.

Where Cross the Crowded Ways of Life

Frank Mason North, 1905

Where cross the crowded ways of life,
Where sound the cries of race and clan,
Above the noise of selfish greed,
We hear thy voice, O Son of Man.

In haunts of wretchedness and need,
On shadow'd thresholds dark with tears,
From paths where hide the lures of greed,
We catch the vision of thy tears.

The cup of cold water giv'n for thee
Still holds the freshness of thy grace;
Yet long these multitudes to see
The sweet compassion of thy face.

O Master, from the mountain side,
Make haste to heal these hearts of pain;
Among these restless throngs abide,
O tread the city's streets again.

Till sons of men shall learn thy love,
And follow where thy feet have trod;
Till glorious from the heavens above,
Shall come the City of our God.

Frank Mason North (1850–1935) was born in New York City. He attended Wesleyan University, graduating in 1872 with an AB. A master's degree followed three years later. He was ordained to the ministry of what was then known as the Methodist Episcopal Church, North, and went on to be pastor of parishes in Florida, New York, and Connecticut before turning to executive work in his denomination. He was editor of a periodical known as

The Christian City and was an official of the New York Church Extension and Missionary Society of the Methodist Church nationally. From 1916–20 he was president of the Federal Council of Churches of Christ in America.[71]

North was, like Gladden, a rational Christian who saw in the prophets and the gospels a mandate to relieve human suffering. Having spent so much of his working life in New York City he did not, however, spend all his time in offices but in walking those city streets to which he would allude in his hymn. When North thought "missionary work," it was not about converting people to a Methodist ideology (if indeed there was ever any such thing) or about saving their souls for eternity. It is clear from the hymn under consideration here that he saw biblical religion and the church that he assumed was committed to its social mandates as the driving force for good here and now.

North's appreciation of the Jesus figure is writ plainly in the hymn text: The Jesus to whom he refers he calls "Master," as perfectly good translation from a form of the Greek word ἐπιστάτης, that is, "chief," "commander," or "master," from ἐπισταμαι, "to understand." North's Jesus understands what North himself understood after walking the streets of Manhattan's lower eastside and experiencing the squalor that must have greeted his eyes, ears, and nose in the latter part of the nineteenth century. North himself, at the pinnacle of his career, went to those places so that he could later write "O Master, from the mountain side, / Make haste to heal these hearts of pain; / Among these restless throngs abide, / O tread the city's streets again."

North's hymn, along with Gladden's *O Master, Let Me Walk with Thee* became the two hymns of Protestantism's social gospel movement, making church attendance ever more relevant to people who thought praising Jesus and worrying about personal salvation could not possibly constitute the be-all and end-all of their religion.

'Tis So Sweet to Trust in Jesus

Louisa M. R. Stead, ca. 1882

'Tis so sweet to trust in Jesus,
Just to take him at His word;
Just to rest upon his promise;
Just to know "Thus saith the Lord."
Jesus, Jesus how I trust him!
How I've proved him o'er and o'er!
Jesus, Jesus, precious Jesus!
O for grace to trust him more
O how sweet to trust in Jesus,
Just to trust His cleansing blood.
Just in simple faith to plunge me
'Neath the healing, cleansing flood! . . .
Yes 'tis sweet to trust in Jesus.
Just from sin and self to cease;
Just from Jesus simply taking
Life and rest and joy and peace . . .
I'm so glad I learned to trust Thee,
Precious Jesus, Savior friend;
And I know that Thou art with me,
Wilt be with me to the end . . .

Louisa M. R. Stead (ca. 1850–1917) was born in Dover, England, and died near Umtali in what was then southern Rhodesia—now Zimbabwe. When she was nine or ten years old, Stead made her confession of faith and began to experience the urge to be a missionary. At about twenty or twenty-one years old, she immigrated to the United States and lived for a time in Cincinnati, Ohio. She was part of a church camp meeting in Urbana, Ohio, some time before 1875—the year of her first marriage to a Mr. Stead—and she signed on to be a missionary to China, but she was adjudged physically unfit for such arduous duty. Meanwhile she gave birth to a daughter, Lily Stead, and after Mr. Stead drowned while attempting to rescue a child in the waters of Long Island Sound—no explanation of what he was doing there—Stead herself took her daughter and went to South Africa to do missionary work. Whilst there she was married again to a native of the continent, one Robert Wodehouse. In the mid-1890s her health began to fail, and the family returned to the United States, where she received critical medical attention and was able to rally. In the early months of the twentieth century, they returned again to Africa, this time to Umtali, where she did missionary work until her retirement in 1911. She lived six more years, dying on January 18, 1917. Her body was buried in a mountainside grave near what had been her home during the last seventeen years of her life.

It is said that, after Stead's demise, the community of black Rhodesians to whom she had ministered for years sang her hymn 'Tis So Sweet to Trust in Jesus in their own tongue:

> Zwakanaka kua Yesu,
> Ku mu kuda ite wo,
> Ku zorora ne ku fara.
> Ne ku siwa iye zwe.
> Yesu, Yesu, ndino imba
> Iye ano ndida wo,
> Yesu, Yesu, wakanaka
> Une nyasha hur wo.[72]

The saccharine passivity of Stead's hymn text does not suggest what must have been the rugged nature of her life—chosen by rather than forced upon her. Despite her off-again, on-again health, she did her work in difficult climes and under circumstances that likewise must have been somewhat primitive compared with her life in Dover and Cincinnati. Intercontinental travel in the nineteenth and early twentieth centuries was not the breeze it is today. What luxury there was in ocean travel was taken on such ships as the Cunard line, which provided for well-heeled passengers going mostly to London or Le Havre. Overland travel on the African continent even in the early twenty-first century is no picnic. One can only imagine how it was in Stead's day. She could not have been all that fragile, but if she was, she was also determined.

Allowing that most hymn texts are poetry and should not be subjected to a strict regime of parsing, it is necessary nonetheless to ask what Stead meant by trusting in Jesus, and, moreover, what or who she meant by "Jesus." The text focuses in its entirety on "Jesus," who except for one reference to the gospels' crucifixion narratives, is this palpable set of embracing arms and strong shoulder on which to lean. The reference to Jesus' death ("Just to trust His cleansing blood. / Just in simple faith to plunge me / 'Neath the healing, cleansing flood!") seems somewhat over-the-top with the plunge into the pool of blood, which, in vivid evangelical imagination, seemed always to be deep as any lake. As has been observed elsewhere in these pages, crucifixion, as grisly and inhumane as it was, generally did not cause the discharge of blood. It is only in John 20:25 that any mention of nails is made, and the only mention of blood comes in 19:34, where a soldier is depicted as thrusting a spear into Jesus' side, causing water and blood to spill out. The crucifixion of a person entailed splaying the body on a cross-piece of wood, with arms bound, usually by leather straps.

The blood atonement that figures so largely in both Catholic and evangelical theology and hence in the kind of hymnody represented by Stead's text, is, at best, a strange doctrine that reflects badly on the imagined deity who would demand such a thing. The story of the near-sacrifice of Abraham's son, Isaac, is writ large in theological arguments about the necessity of sacrifice (cf. Gen 22:1–19).

The truer theme of the hymn comes in these words from the final stanza: "I'm so glad I learned to trust Thee, / Precious Jesus, Savior friend; / And I know that Thou art with me, / Wilt be with me to the end." It may be that such thoughts and sentiments welled up in Stead both in her times of ill-health and in what must have been occasionally difficult times in preaching the gospel, which by her time had become thoroughly European and Westernized and preached to primitive people on a continent as yet uncivilized according to Western standards—not to say that such standards were finally superior to that of the tribes of Southern Rhodesia.

As it happens, the verb "to trust," used over and over in the text, is a better English translation of the New Testament word πίστις (faith), which often turns out to mean a fact-less, sometimes fact-defying determination to believe the incredible. In Homeric Greek, the word has to do with confidence based on experience. Stead trusts "Jesus," but trusts his "word," "promise" and "blood." By his "word," it is reasonable to assume that Stead meant the wisdom of his teaching, especially about how human beings should, for their own good, treat one another, that is, according to the Golden Rule. His "promise" may be a reference to Matt 28:20b, namely, the depiction of the resurrected Jesus uttering his final words to the effect that he will be with his community as long as this world endures. The "blood" she has already mentioned, in that purple locution about plunging into its "cleansing flood."

That plunge is made by such evangelical-minded believers as Stead through a complete surrender of doubt and a confessed "trust in Jesus Christ as a personal savior." The promised result of that was believed to be eternal life in the presence of Jesus in the heavenly realms. Perhaps for Stead, not always physically whole, perhaps not always confident in her own strength, nevertheless going to places far from home to do the work she felt she needed to do, that promise was what kept her going.

Love Lifted Me

James Rowe, 1912

I was sinking deep in sin,
Far from the peaceful shore,
Very deeply stained within,
Sinking to rise no more;
But the Master of the sea
Heard my despairing cry,
From the waters lifted me—
Now safe am I.
Love lifted me, love lifted me,
When nothing else could help,
Love lifted me.
All my heart to Him I give,
Ever to him I'll cling,
In His blessed presence live,
Ever His praises sing.
Love so mighty and so true
Merits my soul's best songs;
Faithful, loving service, too
To Him belong . . .
Souls in danger, look above
Jesus completely saves;
He will lift you by His love
Out of the angry waves.
He's the Master of the sea,
Billows His will obey;
He your Savior wants to be—
Be saved today . . .

James Rowe (1865–1933) was a native of Devonshire, England, and immigrated to the United States when he was twenty-five. He met and married Blanche Clapper of Albany, New York.

He worked for a railroad and then, for a time, as warden of the Hudson River Humane Society. Ever thereafter he made a living by writing song lyrics, editing music magazines, and consulting with several music publishers. Eventually the Rowes moved to Wells, Vermont, where James turned his hand to the composition of verse for greeting card companies. It may be that he wrote nearly nineteen thousand separate pieces of verse for such cards.[73] Rowe clearly had a command of the language and its possibilities of rhyme, reminiscent of W. S. Gilbert of the Gilbert & Sullivan operettas. His daughter who worked with him betimes said, "He delighted in composing extemporaneously a poem of some length to an assembled audience."[74]

Recite to yourself W. S. Gilbert's lyric for the Major-General Stanley from Act I of *The Pirates of Penzance* and note the resemblance in meter and rhyme to the opening line of *Love Lifted Me*:

> Oh, men of dark and dismal fate,
> Forgo your crude employ,
> Have pity on my lonely state.
> I am an orphan boy . . .

There is not much biographical indication of Rowe's religious leanings, much less theological acumen. The continued use of the *Love Lifted Me* hymn in the early twenty-first century seems to be a result of its imagery and catchy rhyming pattern. Rowe could well have heard the story of Jesus and the storm at sea in Matt 14:22–33. In that narrative Jesus is depicted as lifting a sinking Peter from the water and into the boat. The story implies that Peter, who set off on the surface of the water at Jesus' invitation, lost his nerve (faith?) and thus began to sink. If doubt is sin, then Peter "was sinking deep in sin, / Far from the peaceful shore . . . / But the Master of the sea / heard [his] despairing cry / [and] from the waters lifted [him]." It is a rather sophisticated theology that would use the sea's troubled depths as a metaphor for sin. For cultures in antiquity, the sea was believed to be the seat of chaos. It was over such a deep of *tohu v' bohu* (chaos and old night) that the *elohim* were depicted by the writers of Genesis (1:1–2) as moving so as to bring order and purpose to creation.

As with many such hymns of the era, the emphasis is on personal salvation and thus a personal relationship with Jesus. "Love lifted *me*" and "heard *my* despairing cry" (italics added). It is "love" that lifts, Rowe's text says—"love" then being a metaphor for being saved from sin. And if "sin" is doubt and disbelief, then "love" is its antidote, according to Rowe. Love is, in fact, a more attractive approach to religious persuasion than the garden-variety pulpit harangue threatening hell and damnation.

One wonders if Rowe experienced some conversion moment in his life that led him to the composition of this hymn, or whether he was just putting words together in the creative manner that was his wont as a greeting-card message writer. How one could experience love extended by "Jesus" is a question for the psychological-psychiatric profession to plumb—unless one understands that the Jesus figure of the gospels and of Christian systematic theology is a metaphor for human love. Years ago when I was a working journalist covering religion for a major daily newspaper, I had cause to research the work of the late Mother Teresa of Calcutta. She was coming to the American city in which I then worked to set up a convent of her Sisters of the Missionaries of Charity. In the course of that research, I found a copy of an old news photo shot of her. There she was literally lifting up an emaciated man out of a flooding Calcutta gutter. The smile on her face was beatific. The look on his face was one of astonishment. The caption was a single word: LOVE.

O Young and Fearless Prophet

S. Ralph Harlow, ca. 1929

O young and fearless Prophet
of ancient Galilee,
thy life is still a summons
to serve humanity;
to make our thoughts and actions
less prone to please the crowd,
to stand with humble courage
for truth with hearts uncowed.

We marvel at the purpose
that held thee to thy course
while ever on the hilltop
before thee loomed the cross;
thy steadfast face set forward
where love and duty shone,
while we betray so quickly
and leave thee there alone.

O help us stand unswerving
against war's bloody way,
where hate and lust and falsehood
hold back Christ's holy sway;
forbid false love of country
that blinds us to his call,
who lifts above the nations
the unity of all.

Stir up in us a protest
against our greed for wealth,
while others starve and hunger
and plead for work and health;

where homes with little children
cry out for lack of bread,
who live their years sore burdened
beneath a gloomy dread.

O young and fearless Prophet,
we need thy presence here,
amid our pride and glory
to see thy face appear;
once more to hear thy challenge
above our noisy day,
again to lead us forward
along God's holy way.

S. Ralph Harlow (1885–1972) was born in Boston, Massachussetts, to a Congregational minister (Samuel A. Harlow) and his wife Caroline Mudge Usher Harlow. A review of one of his books in the February 26, 1961 New York Times[75] said Harlow studied at Harvard University under William James, received a masters' degree from Columbia University and a PhD from Hartford Theological Seminary. Ordained in the Congregational Church, Harlow taught biblical literature at Smith College. An avowed socialist, he stood for election to Congress in the Second District of Massachusetts and was unsuccessful in three consecutive elections (1932, 1934, and 1936). He was a member of the American Federation of Teachers, the American Association of University Professors, the National Association for the Advancement of Colored People, and the League for Industrial Democracy. He died in Oak Bluffs, Martha's Vineyard, on August 21, 1972, at the age of eighty-seven.

The text of his hymn—especially stanzas three and four— serve as a clear explanation of why the hymn is found in few extant hymnals. It was included in the 1935 and 1964 Methodist Hymnal and the 1966 and 1989 editions of The United Methodist Hymnal. It is not included, for example, in The Hymnal 1982 of the Protestant Episcopal Church.

Harlow's pacifist and socialist inclinations are on display, as is his christology. He used the term "prophet" to account for Jesus, without ever naming him, in the first line of the first stanza, calling him "young and fearless." Harlow, in a possible reference to Luke 9:51,[76] writes of the young and fearless prophet: "thy steadfast face set forward" even though "ever on the hilltop / before [him] loomed the cross." This a militant portrait of Jesus the likes of which we do not see in earlier or later hymns and gospel songs. Gone is the "gentle Jesus, meek and mild," in his place a forthright Amos ready to take on war mongers and nationalists (see stanza three) and political conservatives who would leave the poor as Charles Dickens' Ebenezer Scrooge would leave them, that is, to their own devices even as death threatened: "If they would rather die, they had better do it, and decrease the surplus population."[77]

The phrase "false love of country" must have alienated plenty of church-going people once World War II began and patriotism was reborn. Harlow's picture of Jesus Christ "who lifts above the nations the unity of all" was prescient of what would become the United Nations. He would have a hard go in this the second decade of the twenty-first century as the United States finds itself further isolated from the rest of the world because of its over-the-top support of Israel and its two wars against foes in Muslim nations.

The fourth stanza is reminiscent of the Collect for the Sunday Next Before Advent in the Episcopal prayer book, now out of use: "Stir up, we beseech thee, O Lord, the wills of thy faithful people. . . ."[78] But "stir up in us a protest" presaged the era of protest in the 1960s. Harlow was forthright in his condemnation of greed. What would he have thought of the United States in 2013, when one-percent of the population controls 40 percent of the nation's wealth and where the poor only get poorer, being crowded out of the bottom of the barrel by the collapsing middle class? He pictures the starving and the hungry—an acutely drawn distinction—who "plead for work and health." Could this text of the 1930s be any more applicable to the situation in America at the time of this writing?

Harlow's hymn seems to be out of use altogether in churches where correct theology and liturgy have become the primary concerns and where the interests of denomination executives, parish clergy, and lay leaders focus on the economic bottom line and survival? He returns to the "young and fearless Prophet" image in the final stanza, which must have been Harlow's sense of end-times. He confesses need for the presence of that Prophet amid people's "pride and glory" (whatever he meant by "glory") not to effect salvation by faith but by works "once more to hear thy challenge / above our noisy way, / again to lead us forward / along God's holy way." That "holy way" for Harlow was no gold-paved street in a timeless celestial realm. It was the broken neighborhoods of neglected human beings abiding in want. It was a war-weary world in which swords desperately needed to be beaten into plowshares and spears into pruning hooks.

Harlow gave Christian hymnody a striking new kind of hymn text. He was evidently "less prone to please the crowd" and more inclined "to stand with humble courage for truth," or least for truth as he saw it "with heart uncowed." No wonder the crowd has seemed to have shunned his hymn and the construction of the Christian gospel that he bravely put forth.

In Christ There Is No East or West

William A. Dunkerley, a.k.a John Oxenham, 1908

In Christ there is no East or West,
In him no South or North;
But one great Fellowship of Love
Throughout the whole wide earth.

In him shall true hearts everywhere
Their high communion find;
His service is the golden cord
Close binding all mankind.

Join hands then, brothers of the faith,
What'er your race may be.
Who serves my Father as a son
Is surely kin to me.

In Christ now meet both East and West,
In him meet South and North;
All Christly souls are one in him
Throughout the whole wide earth.

William A. Dunkerley, also known as John Oxenham (1852?–1941), was educated at Victoria University in England, where he was trained in business. Dunkerley adopted "Oxenham" as a nom d'plume but later changed his name altogether. He was one of the best-known poets of his day, a devout churchman, husband, and father. He traveled widely across Europe, South Africa, and America, selling wholesale goods for British firms. He lived for a number of years in France. Eventually he discovered his aptitude as a writer and wrote forty-two novels and twenty-five volumes of poetry. His first poem, which included what became the hymn text, was "Bees in Amber." It was shunned by publishers, so he self-published it shortly before the First World War. It sold more than 285,000 copies. Whilst in the United States in the early 1900s he was recruited to return to England to be the publisher of a weekly edition of the Detroit Free Press published especially for a British readership. During the first world war he wrote and published several volumes of verse for the devotional use of British soldiers. More than a million copies of his books of poetry were in circulation by 1919. The hymn text above is the last entry in a libretto called the "Pageant of Darkness and Light," which was produced from 1908–14 in both Britain and the United States. The hymn text is one of the most optimistic published prior to the war and versifies the highest human hopes against a backdrop of growing mechanized conflict that would shock the civilized world and mark it forever. His *Hymns for Men at the Front* eventually reached eight million copies. Following the war, he wrote a poem entitled "Chaos and the Way Out." It was circulated by the Methodist Church in the United States to its more than twenty thousand congregations for use in a special peace service.[79]

Dunkerley-Oxenham's hymn text is so shot through with optimism and hope that one would be entitled to think he was unaware of the world's precarious state. He was not. The hymn is about Christian unity and does not envision an all-faiths kind of coming together. He was more interested, it seems, in racial and cultural unity and cooperation across the usual barriers. But, of course, there was an East and a West, if only the historic division between Constantinople and Rome ever since 1054 CE. There was a North and South as northern Germany, in particular, became in great part Lutheran in the wake of the Reformation while southern Europe clung to Catholicism. In America the Baptists, Methodists, and Presbyterians became North and South over the slavery and emancipation. There still exists a Southern Baptist Convention. The Episcopalians remained as one even as some of its southern bishops became Confederate generals, yet even this latter church is divided over whether or not the deity can properly be called "You" rather than "Thee," whether women as the vessels of carnal sin can be priests, whether gay and lesbian persons are truly human. Dunkerley-Oxenham was echoing Paul's great optimism, not ever really to be realized: "There is no longer Jew or Greek, there is no longer slave or free, there is no longer male and female, for all of you are one in Christ Jesus" (Gal 3:28; NRSV).

God of Grace and God of Glory

Harry Emerson Fosdick, 1931

God of grace and God of glory, on thy people pour thy power;
Crown thine ancient Church's story; bring her bud to glorious flower.
Grant us wisdom, grant us courage, for the facing of this hour.

Lo! The hosts of evil round us scorn thy Christ, assail his ways!
From the fears that long have bound us free our hearts to faith and praise:
Grant us wisdom, grant us courage for the living of these days.

Cure thy children's warring madness, bend our pride to thy control;
Shame our wanton selfish gladness, rich in things and poor in soul.
Grant us wisdom, grant us courage lest we miss thy kingdom's goal.

Save us from weak resignation to the evils we deplore;
Let the gift of thy salvation be our glory evermore.
Grant us wisdom, grant us courage, serving thee whom we adore.

Used by permission of Elinor Fosdick Downs.

This hymn text is included in this study precisely because it differs in tone, language, and focus from all the above texts save those of Washington Gladden, Frank Mason North, and John Oxenham. The hymn was composed by Harry Emerson Fosdick for the dedication ceremonies of the Riverside Church on Manhattan's Morningside Heights on February 8, 1931. It has become in many ways the theme hymn of progressive Christianity.

Lest it be said that Fosdick abandoned the Second Person of the Trinity in his ministry and in his signature hymn, it will take the reading of only a few pages of an early work of his about the character of Jesus and what Fosdick saw as the importance of the Jesus figure to Christianity and, indeed, to the world, to absolve him of this accusation.[80]

Fosdick was born in 1878 in Buffalo, New York. He earned a bachelor of arts from Colgate University in 1900, a theological degree from Union Theological Seminary, New York City, in 1904, and four years later a master's degree from Columbia University. He began his ministerial career with a nine-year term as pastor of First Baptist Church in Montclair, New Jersey. In 1915 he became the Morris K. Jessup Professor of Practical Theology at Union and was for most of the rest of his life connected in some way with the seminary, which was and remains an outpost for liberal Christianity. From 1918 to 1925 he held the pulpit of the First Presbyterian Church of New York City and, with his 1922 sermon "Shall The Fundamentalists Win?" joined the issue with said fundamentalists over the question of whether the so-called "higher criticism" or the historical-critical method of interpreting the Bible should be adopted, not only by Presbyterians but by all Protestant churches.

Fosdick left the pulpit of First Church at the invitation of John R. Rockefeller, Jr., to become pastor of Park Avenue Baptist Church just as it was beginning its transition to becoming the ecumenical Riverside Church. It was at Riverside that Fosdick realized his vision of a church community whose major function was outreach to those closely contiguous to its location—the academic communities, nearby tenements, and, indeed, the entire population of the northern end of Manhattan Island.

Fosdick had preached a sermon to his Park Avenue Baptist congregation that was eager to move into Riverside saying that it would be "wicked for us to have that new church."

> Whether it is going to be wicked or not depends on what we do with it. We must justify the possession of that magnificent equipment by the service that comes out of it. . . . It is not

settled yet whether or not the new church will be wonderful. That depends on what we do with it. If we should gather a selfish community there, though the walls bulged every Sunday with the congregations, that would not be wonderful.[81]

It was Fosdick's vision that the Riverside Church should be exactly at Frank Mason North's "crowded ways of life / where sound the cries of race and clan" and deeply concerned and involved with the "haunts of wretchedness and need" and standing with open hands and heart on "thresholds dark with fears." Fosdick wanted his congregation corporately to identify with the Jesus Christ about whom he wrote in *The Manhood of the Master* and with him to "tread the city's streets again."

So did he write the dedicatory hymn *God of Grace and God of Glory* in which he referenced "the hosts of evil round us," by which he clearly did not mean the unbelief of heathens. Small doubt that flashing in Fosdick's mind were the twin specters of the Great Depression and the evident helplessness of the Hoover administration to counter them: grinding poverty and bloated greed. Militarism, too, was evil in his sight. Fosdick wrote of "fears that long have bound us," and he could well have meant the narrowness of fundamentalist religion with its scorn of science and rational interpretation of ancient texts. He wrote of being saved—"save us from weak resignation to the evils we deplore." That's what salvation meant to Fosdick.

Thus did his hymn signal a turn toward a rational humanism in American Protestantism, and away from the sound and fury of evangelical biblicism. Fosdick's religion—and his hymn—both were about the community of humankind, not Reginald Heber's "Greenland's icy mountains" or "India's coral strand" nor yet "a palmy plain" to which black Africans supposedly called white Protestants "to deliver their land from error's chain."[82]

Shot through the Fosdick hymn are the stern themes of the parable of the sheep and the goats, of Matt 25:31–36. The glory of this passage is its devotion to the ethical base of Jesus Judaism and to what, finally, is important. It is not doctrine; it is not dogma; it is not right cultic practice. It is human behavior. The sense of the passage is that salvation comes by works or it does not come at all, as in the Epistle of James: "Religion that is pure and undefiled before God the Father is this: to visit orphans and widows in their distress" and, in the same document, "So faith by itself, if it has no works, is dead" (1:27a and 2:17, respectively; NRSV).

One is tempted to rationalize the judgment part of the passage to say that the reward of doing good is in its doing—in other words, consequential. Human experience validates such a rationalization. Matthew had a different idea: Not doing good, that is, omitting to attend to the needs of other human beings, is punishable by death. Jews and Christians are so accustomed to the "thou-shalt-nots" that a "thou-shalt-not-fail-to" comes as a rude surprise. (See Matthew 25:31-46.)

It is an amazing, Dante-esque scene Matthew crafts. It is global in scope and universal in its sweep. It reminds one of Luke's story of Dives and Lazarus in its unforgiving nature. It is in the end just such people as the Lazaruses of this world with their open sores, hollow eyes, and body odor who are to be embraced first, last, and always. If there be privilege, they are the privileged.

From a late first-century CE outlook, this passage would have to be considered admonitory and cautionary. But what it represents is solid evidence that the Jesus Judaism emerging into the Christian church was fundamentally an ethical religion with far less emphasis on the jots and tittles of theology and liturgy than later practice would suggest.

The parable of the sheep and goats furnishes a minor-key finale to a crashing and somewhat dissonant symphony, the final resolution of which will lie somewhere beyond the score and in the lives of those who have heard it and been moved by it. Its effect is stunning and fearsome. Its challenge is daunting but not beyond human understanding for those who summon the nerve to be undaunted. It asks only that human beings look at their weakest and most vulnerable as bosom sisters and brothers. It asks that those with some reach out to those with none, that those with much understand that they must open their hands to those with little—and to do so not as one brushing crumbs from a banquet table, rather as a *maitre d'hotel* provisioning such a table.

Such was Fosdick's vision for his new and last church (he retired in 1946 after fifteen years at Riverside and died in 1969). His vision was that of Matt 25:31–46, in which is spelled out what followers of Jesus must do to be followers. His vision was fulfilled in ways great and small. In an autobiographical work[83] he marveled over the equipage of his magnificent church: "Sometimes visitors, strangers to New York, are mystified and amused by our methods. There are ten kitchens in the church. I have seen many a visitor take for granted such churchly things as Hofmann's lovely pictures and 'the largest carillon in the world,' but ten kitchens!"

Fosdick's religion was neither doctrine nor dogma; it was not right cultic practice. It was humanistic without being a-religious. Riverside needed those ten kitchens to minister to the physical needs of the thousands of people who came through its doors seven days a week for attention to one need or another. They were not by and large the pooh-bahs of the Upper Eastside. They were what the Matthew lection calls "the least of these."

People from all over North America and Europe, and sometimes Africa and Asia, eventually found their ways into the pews of the Riverside Church to hear Fosdick preach. There they heard the message, embodied in *God of Grace and God of Glory*, namely, that the gospel mandates that human beings look at their weakest and most vulnerable as bosom sisters and brothers.

Part III
Hymnody as Theology

Chapter 3

The Theology of the Jesus Hymns

The hymns analyzed above were chosen as representative of a progression of hymnody in nineteenth- and twentieth-century Protestantism. They range in style and taste from the simplicity of *Jesus Loves Me* to the militant *Onward, Christian Soldiers* from the cloying sentiment of *In the Garden* to the glorification of Jesus' instrument of execution in *The Old Rugged Cross* from the straightforward challenge of the social gospel in *Where Cross the Crowded Ways of Life* to, finally, the practical, on-the-ground optimism of *God of Grace and God of Glory.* In each and all—sometimes writ more largely, other times in muted terms—the person of the Jesus figure appears. That character about whom so very little of any reliable history is known but who has dominated Christian thought and theology for two thousand years, is at once friend, victim, savior through substitutional atonement, and master of human endeavor.

What was there about Jesus that so drew the pious to him? It may have been a decision to take the theological cue set out by the author of the Fourth Gospel to the effect that Jesus was the deity in human form. Even though John's "In the beginning was the Word" prologue appeared decades after the narrative gospels with their humanizing stories about Jesus of Nazareth and the infancy narratives of Matthew and Luke, most of the nineteenth- and early twentieth-century hymn writers, even some of the clergy, were probably unaware of the findings of New Testament scholarship to the effect that the Mark was the first of the four canonical gospels, with Matthew, Luke, and John coming later, approximately a decade at a time. Even if they knew the probable order of the gospels' appearances and understood the significance of it, it is doubtful that many hymn writers could discern the complex message of John's prologue, which never mentions Jesus by name. The result is that the writer of the hymn *Tell Me the Stories of Jesus*[84] pretty much accounts for the overall sentiment that carried the American hymn writing enterprise through the nineteenth and into the twentieth centuries. Even the systematic theology that was wrung out of Hebrew and Christian texts is as abstract in the early twenty-first century as it must have seemed 100–150 years ago.

Nonetheless, a deity that could be perceived as a human being, as much as that would stretch ordinary credulity, was manageable and comfortable for those less inclined to philosophical theology than to basic, down-to-earth religion based on stories about a baby worshipped by both shepherds and magi that made people think of kings; about a bar mitzvah-aged boy who mixed it up in the Temple courtyard with learned scholars; about a young man who submitted to a baptism for the forgiveness of sins "to fulfill all righteousness" and about his self-exile to the wilderness, there to be tested by the devil; about one who seemed to have mastered the literature of his religion and was not embarrassed to teach from it and to act upon it; about that teacher who could also heal the sick and make the blind see, the deaf hear and the lame walk, all the while on the go with "no place to lay his head"; about his willingness to confront and be confronted by power; about his passive resistance to persecution; about his willingness to die so that others might live; and about how he rose from the grave and became known to those who had followed him in life. That is why many of the better known Protestant hymns that are used still in the early twenty-first century are centered on Jesus rather than on the other two persons of theology's "holy trinity." "No one has ever seen God. It is God, the only Son . . . who has made Him known" (John 1:18; NRSV). "The wind (spirit) blows where it chooses, and you hear the sound of it, but you do not know where it comes from or where it goes" (John 3:8a; NRSV). Every teacher of creative writing has hammered home the dictum "write what you know." The hymn writers wrote what they thought they knew. Their perception of their own religious conviction centered on him and the stories about him they had learned in Sunday school, at their mothers' knees, in the warp and woof of devotional life that helped form their beliefs.

The Jesus they "knew," as was discussed in Chapter 2, surely was a not a single actual person, as elementary New Testament scholarship has handily demonstrated. "Jesus" is in effect a blank canvass stretched on a frame, a pallet—paint pots and brushes at the ready—with tentative sketches spread upon easels representing other would-be artists' attempts to account for him. Every preacher or Sunday school teacher or inquirer ends up painting the picture of the Jesus he or she perceives or desires. The basic material is in the sketches known as the gospels and the stories that trail away from them into even more surmise. Thus, the Jesus of the hymns has become a collage of many colors and textures representing different convictions and aspirations.

Jesus as Protector, Comforter, Surrogate Spouse

These were familiar characterizations of Jesus that hymn writers have employed. They touched the sentiments of lonely and troubled persons who were perceived as seeking refuge and comfort as if in the arms of a lover, a spouse, or any strong and reliable supporter who would coddle the lonely and troubled one on the breast, arm around him or her implying safety from trouble, freedom from worry, relief from troubling thoughts and fears. The protector and comforter is, however, a way station on the road to heaven and eternal life, which was and is imagined as a state of being in which no comfort or protection would be necessary—comfort and protection being the essence of that state. It is why in the literature of piety, heaven is called "home." About the only reference to an embracing Jesus is found in Mark 10:16, and it has to do with children. Mark depicts Jesus taking them in his arms and making a blessing over them. It is of interest that neither Matthew nor Luke, both of whom included in their narratives parallels of the Markan passage, omitted reference to the embrace. But the depiction in one verse of eight words, all of one syllable, has been repeated in stained glass windows and in countless illustrations for Sunday school literature. It is the "gentle Jesus, meek and mild" of Charles Wesley's 1763 hymn that pleads for surcease "fast in Thine embrace." That Jesus is a favorite of the Protestant piety of the nineteenth and early twentieth centuries.

That sentiment was no doubt a commentary upon the life that many Christians lived. Those who worshipped in the small-town or out-in-the-country churches before the days of the telephone and radio were likely to have experienced loneliness and isolation. They had to rely on the companionship of marriage and parenthood for emotional support and security, with no guarantee they would gain either while knowing they had little choice but to stick it out. They may have heard hellfire and damnation in their preachers' sermons—and probably expected it as a decent substitute for having to endure the real thing—but they heard and sang the hymns about the comforting, protecting Jesus who, they hoped, would have the last word in this life and the next. It was a Jesus almost completely of the imaginative yearning, and it was that Jesus who kept a lot of people going when everything else seemed arrayed against them. "Jesus, keep me near the cross," Fanny Crosby wrote, meaning, we might suppose, that Jesus' suffering was only greater and of infinitely greater significance than anything she or any other human being might experience. But her belief and that of myriad Christians was that Jesus, while suffering and dying, was vindicated in his resurrection. And not only that, but St. Paul had promised that "just as Christ was raised from the dead by the glory of the Father, so we too might walk in newness of life" (Rom 6:4a; NRSV).

The elements of belief are in many respects unrelated to the church's theology. Belief, such as expressed in the texts of several of the hymns treated of in this book, has its roots as much in personal need as in orthodoxy. The image of being gathered into the arms of an incarnate deity and in such an embrace being protected from the exigencies of normal human life, is nowhere suggested in the church's historic creeds, though it can be limned from the appropriation to oneself of such biblical passages as Psalm 23. The passage is a poetic image that acknowledges the valley of the shadow of death and the presence of enemies. Yahweh is imagined as a shepherd leading a sheep of his flock to pasture and running water, through the valley and out the other side. Or: "He shall feed his flock like a shepherd; he shall gather the lambs with his arm, and carry them in his bosom, and shall gently lead those that are with young" (Isa 40:11; NRSV). Try to hear that text as rendered in Movement 20 of G. F. Handel's *Messiah*, the double aria for alto and soprano, to get its full impact.

Many of the writers of the hymns under consideration in this book lived before the insights of Sigmund Freud and Carl Jung were incorporated into psychological and psychiatric therapy. It is not difficult to see how the phenomenon of transference—an interior process by which one displaces a set of feelings generally associated with a normally appropriate person to another who, given the relationship, is not an appropriate recipient of those feelings when physically or verbally expressed—was at work in the earnest piety of such hymns as those that depicted Jesus as the comforter, even as the therapist to whom one could tell anything and from whom one could expect succor. The hymn *In the Garden* imagines Jesus talking with one who places himself in the garden of resurrection and there encounters Jesus: "And He walks with me, and He talks with me, and tells me I am His own." The hymn writer Jeremiah Rankin, as we have seen, put it this way: "Are you weary, are you heavy-hearted? Tell it to Jesus, / Tell it to Jesus; Are you grieving over joys departed? / Tell it to Jesus alone." An observant and knowledgeable Roman Catholic might be able to make the connection between that sentiment and the confession of his sins to a priest on the other side of the confessional, standing in for Jesus or for whatever person of the Trinity the priest is the surrogate.

The inescapable conclusion is that in such hymns as are being considered in this book, it is the personal, individual aspect that seems paramount. Not many uses of "we" or "our" appear in the hymn texts. It is "I," "me," and "mine." Yet the ethos of the Christian church in most of its incarnations from its most primitive years until recent times was communal. The community was the seat and focus of the practice of Christianity. Baptism, of course, became an individual thing, but it focused on the initiation of the candidate into the life of the community. Yet evidence exists to the effect that baptisms were often by households in the primitive church. The baptism of the head of a household gathered all who were part of it under the umbrella of salvation. The story of the baptism of Cornelius (Acts 10:47–48) strongly suggests it was a general baptism of all in the household, from elders to slaves. Three clear cases of household baptisms named in the New Testament include the households of Lydia (Acts 16:15), the Philippian jailor (Acts 16:33–34) and Stephanus (1 Cor 1:16).

As the church matured, baptism became more and more a sacrament focused on individuals until in recent times it, along with confirmation, became the infant version of the Jewish bar and bat mitzvahs. How odd it is that so-called christening and the galas that follow it are celebrated for infants and very young children who have such insufficient powers of reason and facility for memory that they will never be able to recall the act or their participation in the hoopla surrounding it.

By the time the Separatists defined the initiation rite as "adult believer baptism," the journey from community to individual was completed, thus paving the way for the intense piety of the "I" and "me" hymns that are still sung and heard in Protestant churches, particularly those of the evangelical movement.

Jesus as Friend, Companion on the Way, and Good Buddy

"What a friend we have in Jesus," wrote Joseph Scriven, "all our sins and griefs to bear." At least he didn't write, "What a friend I have in Jesus." But it is an intimate "we" Scriven uses, meaning any individual can claim Jesus as a friend—an interesting concept. Jesus as teacher, Jesus as shepherd, Jesus as leader, Jesus as healer, but Jesus as "friend?" The word "friend" appears fifteen times in the New Revised Standard Version of the New

Testament, thirteen of which are in the gospels. It is used of Jesus twice, at Matt 11:19 with a parallel at Luke 7:34, naming him as "a friend of toll collectors and sinners." The word "friend" in these places means that Jesus was thought to have consorted, eaten with, and otherwise had pleasant relationships with that ilk. It does not suggest that they were on personally intimate terms. At John 11:11, Jesus is made to refer to Lazarus as "our friend" who "has fallen asleep." Otherwise there are no depictions of Jesus sitting in deep, companionable conversations with anyone. So what made Scriven think that Jesus was "our friend" in the sense that we could transfer our guilt, our sorrows, our "needless pain" on to him? As has been pointed out, C. Austin Miles in his *In the Garden* depicts himself in conversation with the risen Jesus who "walks with me and talks with me." Such a sentiment is born of individual need and desire rather than a reading of texts. This is not to say that the texts are any final word, but they do represent what record—if it is a record—we possess of how those who lived in what would have been the biblical Jesus' time appreciated him. Of course, the biblical record is varied and undependable in terms of the person of Jesus, of who he might have been, of his nature and disposition, and so on.

Wishful longing is at the base of the kind of piety with which we deal in such hymns as *What a Friend We Have in Jesus*. It may mean that the composer, if he or she was writing from experience, felt there was no one to trust with "sins and griefs," no one on whom to lean for comfort and encouragement. But for one immersed to whatever degree in the language and concepts of nineteenth- and twentieth-century Protestant religion, it was possible to turn to those extra-historical figures of biblical legend and myth, and that deity alleged to have put on human vesture. One did not need to make an appointment with him, travel one inch from where one stood in that time of need, or explain what or why. One needed only to approach him through the medium of prayer, believing that the intentional thought or its expression in words would get through to him and that, because the assumption is that "God is love," he would somehow respond to the prayer—though the thoughtful pray-er would hedge the bet by quoting Jesus as depicted in Gethsemane by Matthew (at 26:42), Mark (at 14:36), and Luke (at 22:42), as saying in effect, "But whatever you want, God."

So commonplace have the concept and the practice of prayer become that, while we might look twice at a person addressing a lamp post in earnest conversation, we do not blink an eye when we see a person kneeling in a church, head bowed and supposedly praying. We know the lamp post is not listening, is incapable of listening. Do we know that neither the inner space of that church nor its fixtures are capable of listening to the pray-ers' petitions, whether merely thought rather than mouthed? What is the difference between the lamp post and the church edifice? Is the practice not delusional in nature either way?

When we observe or are part of a large gathering of people speaking or singing in unison some petition to an unseen deity, are we less likely to call it delusional because it is a communal act? Do Muslims at their five-times-daily prayer or the minyan at its prayers, or the monks at matins and vespers, address a friend in the Holy Prophet, the *elohim,* or the deity that Christ embodied? That is probably not what is intended in any of those cases. One speaks to a friend casually and informally, even off-handedly. One who wants to keep a friend tries not to ask him or her for the impossible. One does not cast all one's fears and doubts and troubles upon a friend who may have plenty of his own. A rational adult does not do any of that sort of thing with or to an imaginary or, at the least, invisible friend. So to speak or write of the Jesus or Jesuses of the gospels and the stories that derive from them as a "friend" is to presume the irrational and to ignore what testimony there is, however tainted by imagination—wholesale and retail—by mythology and just plain wishful longing.

This phenomenon is accounted for in striking terms by psychological anthropologist T. M. Luhrmann in a 2012 book *When God Talks Back: Understanding the American Evangelical Relationship with God.* Luhrmann lived for a significant time among contemporary evangelicals and described in detail how it was that they believed utterly and without a doubt in the nearness of God, so much so that they would "have coffee with God," going so far as to set an extra cup on the table to lubricate the conversation.

Luhrmann writes of a pastor of a church she attended for some time who, she said, "explicitly encouraged us to experience God as a friend. . . . He encouraged us to set out a second cup of coffee for God in the morning—to pour God an actual cup of steaming coffee, to place it on an actual table, and to sit down at that table with our own mug to talk to God about things on our minds."[85]

It is such a friend folks have in Jesus. That friend can be compared not only to a coffee-drinking partner but also to a child's teddy bear or Linus VanPelt's security blanket.[86] It is like the imaginary Santa Claus to whom the innocent child writes a Christmas letter requesting this toy or that in strong hopes of getting that very thing. When there is no provident parent or relative to provide the longed-for object, the child is crushed—but at the same time learns the hard lesson that asking is not tantamount to receiving, neither knocking to opening, nor seeking to finding.

Those are harsh words on such a tender topic as prayer in a culture where respect for the beliefs, however incredible, of the other is expected. The honest psychiatrist will call that kind of prayer delusional and even dangerous. One does not want the pilot of his aircraft to bow his head in prayer and ask a god for a safe flight. One wants the pilot to know that his craft is flight-worthy in every respect, that his skills are the highest possible and honed to the task at hand, that he has checked and re-checked the weather and the availability of air lanes, that he has been assured of a safe place to land the craft upon arrival at the destination.

What a friend we have in human potential, skill, and its application to the appropriate task.

Jesus as Substitutionary Victim

The words "blood," "bleeding" and "bled" appear thirteen times in the twenty-eight hymns under consideration in this book, plus other metaphors—some obvious, some not—for blood and its shedding. There are no fewer than forty direct references to the blood of Jesus in the twenty-seven documents of the New Testament, and many more indirect references. The direct references appear four times in Matthew, once in Mark, twice in Luke, five times in John, twice in Acts, twice in Romans, thrice in 1 Corinthians, once in Colossians and twice in Ephesians, ten times in Hebrews, twice in 1 Peter, four times in 1 John and twice in the Revelation. One would expect much mention of blood in the crucifixion narratives, though in the usual Roman crucifixions, victims were bound with leather fetters to the rood and left to die of exposure, exhaustion and asphyxiation, not so often of flesh wounds.

But sacrifice as a necessary ritual had been part of the religions of the ancient Near East for as many as four to five thousand years before the Common Era. From the earliest times of the Hebraic experience, sacrifice was one of its central and dominant themes. The destruction of the Second Temple in 70 CE brought an abrupt end to animal sacrifice at the hands of priests, and has never been practiced since by any authentic branch of Judaism. Nevertheless, its centrality and dominance is reflected over and over again in the Hebrew scriptures and spilled over into those of Christianity. The sacrifices are both expiatory and substitutionary—the first serving as an apology to the law-giving deity for disobeying its commandments, the second being the willing offering of a victim on behalf of others—the victim, in the case of Jesus Christ, assumed to be sinless so that his self-sacrifice is as that of an innocent lamb. The deity is righteous and demands righteousness. "The wages of sin is death," said St. Paul (Rom 6:23a; NRSV). Certain theologians argue that human sin must somehow be atoned for, or God is mocked. And, as St. Paul also declared, "God is not mocked" (Gal 6:7; NRSV). Such theology reverberated through nineteenth- and early twentieth-century American Protestantism and is echoed still in many evangelical churches and, one supposes, all fundamentalist churches. It is therefore no surprise that the language and its graphic images are so often found in such hymn texts as we have analyzed.

What may be the *locus classicus* of that particular piece of theology is found in Hebrews: "Without the shedding of blood there is no forgiveness of sins" (9:22b; NRSV). If one starts at this point and connects the dots on the vast canvas that is systematic theology, the pattern is quickly seen: The Adam-Eve myth followed by the Cain-Abel myth with their transgressions of direct disobedience and fratricide led to what the Genesis writer describes as the "wickedness of humankind on the earth" and Yahweh's sorrow at having created human beings and his decision to wipe them out completely (6:5ff; NRSV). Comes then the great flood meant to purify creation, Noah and his clan spared because he was deemed righteous. But of course, Noah, being human, went on post-Ark to produce descendants who are implicated in the story as attempting to build a tower to the heavens and thus become gods, maybe even to supplant Yahweh. One of those descendants, the genealogy in the text suggests, was Abram, later Abraham. Perhaps Abraham's guilt at casting out Hagar and her child upon the demand of Sarah was echoed in the *elohim* ordering Abraham to make a burnt sacrifice of Isaac. It seems clear that human sacrifice was practiced in Israel's earlier times. The strange omission of Isaac's name in Gen 22:19, which says that Abraham went back to his entourage, suggests that some earlier version of the story concluded with the sacrifice of Isaac. James L. Kugel, chair of the Institute for the History of the Jewish Bible at Bar Ilan University in Israel and the Harry M. Starr Professor Emeritus of Classical and Modern Hebrew Literature at Harvard University, thinks that ancient Israelites, like other tribes and clans of the time, practiced child sacrifice.[87] Mark S. Smith, Skirball Chair of Bible and Ancient Near Eastern Studies in the Department of Hebrew and Judaic Studies at New York University, seems to think that as late as 800 BCE child sacrifice was accepted and performed in the name of Yahweh.[88] Isa 30:27–33 certainly makes Yahweh look like a deity eager to smell the flesh of burning victims.

With that as background, those Jews still connected to the ancient tradition but moving away from it into splinter groups formed around the ethical teachings attributed to Jesus, felt required to turn the execution of their hero as a criminal into a sacrifice. They couldn't say that Rome had Jesus burned at the stake, though it is fairly clear that Polycarp of Smyrna perished as a martyr about 120 years after Jesus would have been executed. But because crucifixion was in the first-century CE Rome's preferred means of torture and humiliation, which often enough caused death, the story is that Jesus' death was the result of crucifixion. Nero was a specialist at this. Tacitus (*Annals* XV.44) suspected Christians were not only nailed to crosses but then set afire as well.

A couple of decades before the evangelists began assembling their crucifixion accounts, St. Paul had already created the beginnings of a soteriology based on the crucifixion. Paul would say to the Romans that "Christ died for us" and that "we have been justified [or made right] by his blood" (5:8–9; NRSV). Paul said also that those who have sinned "are now justified by [God's] grace as a gift, through the redemption that is in Christ Jesus, whom God put forward as a sacrifice of atonement by his blood" (3:24–25; NRSV). At 1 Cor 15:3 (NRSV), Paul says "Christ died for our sins in accordance with the scriptures." Thus the die is cast, and when in the next generation Jesus Jews on their way to becoming Christians would begin to hear and perhaps to read the stories of that death, they would come to see Jesus' death not as the result of Roman execution but of God's doing. They may have known of the liturgical hymn Paul quoted in his epistle to the churches in Philippi: "Think as Jesus thought—he who, though he was the perfect form of God did not consider that as something to take personal advantage of, but let all that go and became as a slave, having already been born a human being. And as such, he submitted to reality and conceded the inevitability of his choice and went willingly to his death on a cross" (2:5–11).

Thus was what theologians came to call the "substitutionary atonement" firmly established in doctrine. Even though blood sacrifice was a thing of the past by the time the nineteenth- and early twentieth-century Protestant hymn texts were written, it was fixed in place by the literal interpretation of the Bible. Dear to many evangelical preachers unto this day are the Pauline texts cited above. The preaching of them can be effective and power-ful, engendering guilt and the desire to somehow "make it up to God." Catholicism wields that power through the sacrament of confession and the threat of excommunication. Protestantism uses it to set up its own kind of priesthood in which the clergy command the attention of congregations with forthright sermons about the need to "get right with God," and so on and so forth. The cross is everywhere as a symbol of both of those expressions of Christianity. A preacher will be raising funds and will be wont to say something like this, "Can't you give just 100 dollars to (fill in the blank here) for Christ who died for you?" If that preacher sticks to his guns on the threat of damnation for the unbelieving or unrepentant, the image of the sacrificed Christ is potent. The "blood" hymns, sung robustly and often enough, underscore that image.

Jesus as Mentor and Guide

As the higher criticism slowly entered the bloodstream of American theological education, its students and future clergy began to see the Jesus figure in a different light—no longer neces-sarily the agent of salvation by blood atonement but as a moral and spiritual lodestar. The gospels were mined for examples of what the evangelists may have said or hinted at about his disposition toward other human beings. In fact, Jesus was be-coming less and less a victim of an inevitable process of paying for human sin with his own broken body and shed blood, but more and more one from whom, through study and prayer, one might obtain guidance to daily living and longer-term survival as a child of God. One hymn in particular (Edward Hopper's 1871 *Jesus, Savior, Pilot Me*) envisioned Jesus as the keeper of the chart and compass by which one could navigate his or her way through "life's tempestuous sea." In Hopper's poetry, there were "unknown" and "boisterous waves" along with "hiding rock and treacherous shoal." The idea was to complete the voyage to the shore—metaphors for life and death—in the wholeness of faith.

That compelling image of Jesus as sea pilot has survived in the common practice of millions of Christians who are not embarrassed to say that they have "prayed about" what they should do faced with one kind of decision or another. It is a piety of consultation with a higher power in which the Jesus figure is neither a righteous judge nor an intentional victim, nor yet a remote figure of the theologians' Holy Trinity. Rather, he is a caring, older brother just out of sight but not out of human hearing—one who can hear, will hear and will somehow, through a mental process unknown to scientists, help petitioners decide what to do or say, not do or not say. To say that such a thing requires the suppression of incredulity is to say the obvious. Whence the idea that a dead wisdom teacher or a resurrected victim or a victorious and ascended lord is able or willing to hear the individual petition for guidance? Does it come from the sparrows and the hairs of Matt 10:29–30? Or Psalm 23?

Two churches within a ten-minute drive from the study in which this manuscript was written are typical of many that are farther away. One advertises a weekly "prayer conference," which, as I understand it, is run along the lines of an Alcoholics Anonymous meeting. People are invited to come, sit in a circle and share their "prayer concerns," accept advice from veteran pray-ers along the lines of what will eventually be communally addressed to the deity. I have heard it said that people frequently come away from such sessions with clarity about their confusion. I am also told that God is particularly addressed as "Jesus." It is said that Jesus is invisibly at hand and further that it is as he himself is said to have promised: "Truly I tell you, if two of you agree about anything you ask, it will be done for you. . . . For where two or three are gathered in my name, I am there among them" (Matt 18:19–20; NRSV).

The other church has lawn signs on either side of its driveway asking: "May we pray for you?" A prayer-box stands near the front door. The idea seems to be that if you don't have the time to "take it to the Lord in prayer," the people inside will. The expectation seems to be that an answer to an anonymous prayer processed by the pray-ers inside will somehow reach the too-busy-to-pray petitioner with the requested guidance. The theology that seems to underlie these ideas may spring from the hypothesis of the immanent deity, to wit: that the powers that be in the universe also dwell within every atom, yea, proton and neutron of same, are present in all times and in all places simultaneously. You could reasonably conclude that, on the basis of such a theological proposition, those powers already knew what you needed before you knew it and might have been willing to provide it. On the one hand, that would seem to fly in the face of free will, and on the other the supposed goodness of those powers known to some as God. Mark Twain is said to have been ever so slightly critical of God for noticing that a sparrow fell but apparently did nothing to stop the fall, neither to ease it nor afterward to succor it.

As defiant of logic as it is, as bereft of any testable data, the theology and piety of the ever-present, open-line, "call now, operators are standing by" Jesus at the ready to guide the emotionally needy through one crisis or decision or another is likely to be with us evermore. It could be said that it is a harmless thing, though there are those who would argue that it is also dangerous. One of the upsides of the "prayer concerns conferences" noted above is that at least the individual pray-er has the opportunity to discuss his or her prayer with others and could, if suffering a somehow perverse or suggested mental imbalance, be persuaded to seek another kind of help.

Jesus the Confessor and Therapist

How much of a qualitative distance is it from the group prayer, AA-like session to the confessional booth of such communions as either require or offer the sacrament of penance, which usually involves one priestly minister and one penitent, or yet to the counselor's inner sanctum or the analyst's couch? The hymn writer Jeremiah Rankin suggested that you can simply *Tell It to Jesus*—in ritual language, the confessor; in psychological/psychiatric language, the therapist. This is akin to the individual petition to the accessible Jesus, but it is by nature a more intimate idea. Rankin says that Jesus is "a friend that's well-known" and that one has "no other such a friend or brother" so you can "tell it to Jesus alone." One searches the literary tradition for the one-

on-one human-and-divine instance: Genesis 32 and Jacob's wres-
tling with "one," whom the writer of the passage clearly thought
of as the *elohim*; Exodus 3 and Moses at Horeb encountering the
elohim in the burning bush that was not burnt; 1 Kings 18 and
Elijah meeting Yahweh in the thin sound of silence; Isaiah 6 and
the future prophet's aural encounter with the bidding voice of
Yahweh; Jeremiah 1ff and that prophet's account of his argument
with Yahweh; Luke 22 and Jesus in that final colloquy with his
Father—all for example.

Rankin's text does not invite the interrogation or challenging
of the deity, but only spilling it all out to Jesus, whose presence
and attention are taken for granted. One must traverse a broad
expanse of assumption to get to the point at which the figure
variously presented in the New Testament documents is or can
be that therapist or confessor. The idea may be that Jesus has seen
it all. If you can take the various gospel data as data, you can say
that he had lived in poverty; that he was called to a difficult mission; that he was both admired and reviled; that he was arrested,
convicted (some say unjustly) of a capital crime and that he was
executed. And the story is that he came back from that death to
tell his disciples that he would be with them always, even to the
close of the age.

So if all that or even part of it were true, why couldn't the
person troubled by his self-perceived sins or unresolved troubles
"tell it to Jesus"? You can do it under the seal through the good
offices of the priest and receive not only counsel but penance, as
well as comfort, guidance and an opportunity to unburden yourself with impunity. Or you may feel free to go directly to Jesus in
the form of personal petition, obviously somehow believing that
his is a real, ready, and receptive ear. My granddaughter, Grace,
when she was maybe four or five, had obviously internalized a
Daily Vacation Bible School dictum: "Don't be afwaid, just be-
wieve." As, at this writing, Grace has passed her twelfth birthday
and is well on her way to her thirteenth, her appreciation of reality will surely have changed—mostly because she may be one of
the smartest people I have yet to know. She seems to me to be

the kind of human being who will, yes, trust, but also verify. So I don't know at this time whether or not Grace would "tell it to Jesus alone" or would seek out one of her parents, her sister, her pastor—or even her aging and agnostic grandfather—but more likely the one she once called "Gamma," to tell whatever she thought needed to be told.

The Jesus to whom one can tell everything is clearly an invention of a brand of nineteenth-century Christian piety in search of a listening ear and sympathetic heart. The idea is more a product of human need than of the paucity of real information about who "Jesus" may have been and what he may have done. That should come as no surprise, because a patient examination of the gospels—canonical and otherwise—reveals that their narratives concerning "Jesus" vary widely in their attempts to account for him. It is either a case of different people looking at the lore of the same person through different lenses and needs, or it is a case of different people looking at different persons through those same lenses and needs.

Withal, the figure of the welcoming Jesus willing to hear it all told and willing to forgive, if not forget, has remained part of the structure of Christian piety well into the twenty-first century. It is in a way the triumph of the piety of another time. It is, in fact, a part of "that old-time religion" that's still good enough for plenty of people. Even so, it has the effect of deeply individualizing religion and making it an enterprise of singular personal effort. The fact is that many human difficulties, problems, failures, and unaccomplished goals and aims are the kind of unhappiness and unfulfillment shared in some part by almost every person alive. No one is ever an unqualified success, or at least not for very long. A new piety might be the realization that we are all in this together, as the saying goes, and that telling those we can see, rather than the Jesus we cannot, of those things that plague us might issue in new life. Such a sentiment was caught up in the text of a post-Vatican II hymn that became popular not only in Roman Catholic but other congregations in the late 1960s and 1970s: *And They'll Know We Are Christians by Our Love.*[89] Such knowledge, the text says, will proceed from evidence that those singing it have covenanted to work side by side to guard every person's dignity and pride.

Jesus: Object of the Needy

Somehow the Jesus of the gospel narratives and of systematic theology was turned into an object of personal need, and that by such hymns as Annie Sherwood Hawks' *I Need Thee Ev'ry Hour*. She pleads in its text for the 24/7 presence of Jesus in her life in the way a mystic confesses that he senses the immanence of God in all things at all times. If Hawks' prayer in music is a plea for that, then she was substituting the "Jesus" of the gospels for that numinous experience of which desert ascetics have ever told. Lovers and spouses are wont to say that they "need" each other, and in many different ways. Neither lovers nor spouses stay together very long if their lives are bound up in 24/7 spatial immediacy. They need to think of themselves individually and do for themselves individually and bring such thoughts and deeds to their periodic meeting places, whether at the dinner table, in the den and in bed. Need for the other is a healthy urge, but neediness soon becomes an intolerable burden on the needed.

Whence the kind of sentiment that unabashedly confesses such need? The answer must lie in the life of the person who confesses it. Jesus is at best a composite figure of first-century CE lore, a persona, almost, a blank canvas upon which anyone can paint a likeness to suit himself or herself—and millions have, all the way from Michelangelo to Caravaggio to Warner Sallman to the stick figures limned by Sunday school children. The Jesus figure has been romanticized to the point of saccharine satiation, no less in hymns in which the name is mentioned. Even the slightest application of rational criticism must come to the conclusion that the Jesus who is needed "every hour" is a substitute for someone or something perceived by the one in need as missing in his or her life. Either that, or such hymnists as Hawks were fixated on an image of a savior that could and would answer her plea to materialize across the abyss of the ages to hover over her in times of temptation, pain, and hurt. "No tender voice like thine can peace afford."

In a rational world, people who hear voices of the dead or of a so-called "spirit world," or wish to hear them must be adjudged as bordering on delusion. Yet so common is the sentiment of "needing Jesus" that it has become acceptable and, in some venues, desirable. Almost as a matter of course some people speak the name of "Jesus" aloud when they experience moments of stress or anticipation. It becomes almost a verbal amulet or rabbit's foot, as in Lydia Odell Baxter's hymn *Take the Name of Jesus with You*. She advised others to "take it . . . where'er you go" for joy and comfort on the way, as a shield. She called it a "precious" name. What could she have meant in so writing? If we consider that in the Hebrew tradition the word name means "nature" or "disposition," one possible meaning might be that one should take the nature of Jesus upon oneself—that nature being, supposedly, the inclination to give of self, to truth-tell and to include rather than exclude. However, it is doubtful that Baxter meant anything like that. Few people in Baxter's time sharing her piety would have gone that far. For her and for those who sang her hymn, Jesus' name thought of, meditated on, spoken aloud, or worn like armor constituted a sense of religious superiority, of hope with an eye to everlasting life. In any event, that Jesus was "needed" and claimed by people of such piety. He or his name fulfilled a definite and enduring longing for something other than what the material world could or would provide.

It is not wrong to wonder if such sentiment signaled the lack of sexual fulfillment or the absence of any kind of lasting intimacy. One is almost tempted to apply the sense of 1 John 4:20 to the effect that it is the more obvious thing to love those who can be seen rather than those who can't, those in evidence rather than those who are imaginary. How would Baxter and others who share her piety and who profess belief in an unseen and invisible Jesus know that he was near? What objective data would they offer to demonstrate it? Would they attempt to invoke that presence in a prison cell whilst visiting one imprisoned, or in a collective bargaining picket of a corporation whose executives are economically abusing their workers? How would they attempt to convince those in such situations that they "need" Jesus or should "take" his name where and however they go? What would they say to Jews or Muslims or Hindus or Buddhists or unbelievers? Is "Jesus" an idea that goes with the practice of the Christian religion, or is he at the point of the missionary spear meant to pierce the flesh of other religions and cultures?

In a free society, especially set in a nation wherein the freedom of religion and its free exercise are taken together as a given, one can believe in and preach and write hymns about any religious figure one wants. And there is no requirement that any of it make sense. It seems evident even or especially in this era of momentous changes in climate patterns, international political currents, and astounding advances in communication that an "old-time religion" mentality is still alive and is still well—built up, perhaps, by the need of people to latch on to something or someone that is redolent of an allegedly simpler past when things were surer. The Jesus of many hymns, as unconnected as that figure is with the portrayal of him in the gospels and the accounting of him in christology, seems to be part of the past people dismayed by the present are trying to recreate. It is easier to whisper, "Jesus, Jesus," than to try to make sense of algorithms, unmanned drones, the nihilism of al Qaeda, and the unpredictable cant and hypocrisy of politics.

Jesus: Object of Desire

Adelaide Pollard's 1902 hymn *Have Thine Own Way, Lord* was analyzed above both for its theology and its emotion. It was suggested that some of its language bordered on the sexual. And that is no great matter. Why should not the natural urges and feelings of sexuality be discerned in religious emotion? Psychologists and psychiatrists have spoken of transference; ask any parish minister who engages in pastoral counseling. He or she will tell you that it happens all the time because the pastor is a) in a position of power and b) because the pastor is at his or her best entirely gentle and emotionally accessible to the counselee. Most of Pollard's life was lived before what is now called "pastoral counseling" became a regular feature of ministerial life. How much actual theological education Pollard had is not known. What is known, as William J. Reynolds wrote, was that she was "strangely attracted to extreme religious sects and groups"[90] and was at one time associated with an evangelist who made a name for himself predicting the imminent return of Christ. It appears that Pollard was suggestible and vulnerable. She had a strong relationship with an evangelist named Alexander Dowie, but no other men are mentioned in the minimal data about her life. Of frail health most of her life, she could rely on the "Lord" of whom she wrote the hymn not to attempt anything overt with her frail frame, as he was invisible and non-corporeal—or at least he would be until his Second Coming.

Jesus as Personal Hero

There is abroad in the seemingly endless image world of Jesus Christ the idea that he is a hero who reaches down or out to rescue any one in danger. Plenty of human beings have been in danger, and many of them have perished over time without rescue. Thus the question must be asked, why would a figure believed to be in some part or wholly divine only rescue the perishing here and there, now and then? A different kind of saving hero is one who offers guidance, who is a scout or a pilot. One can follow his proffered directions or not. Edward Hopper's hymn *Jesus, Savior, pilot me* strikes that tone, portraying Jesus as one with both chart and compass and, presumably, the seamanship necessary to avoid "hiding rock, and treacherous shoal." The implication is that Hopper's image of Jesus is of one having divine discernment not available to human beings and power to use it to save the earnest petitioner from what might well consume the non-petitioner. Rank upon rank of theologians have envisioned God the Father as the omniscient and omnipotent one. Why did Hopper choose to make Jesus the pilot and the holder of the chart and compass—both of these presumably standing for omniscience? In nineteenth-century Christian piety in America, the human-divine Jesus was the accessible one. Relatively few people had attained the appreciation of the known world and of the universe that wider immersion in the physical sciences would afford. Charles Darwin's *The Origin of Species* had only been in print for a dozen years before the composition of Hopper's hymn text. And it would be another three decades before Albert Einstein loosed his Theories of Relativity on the world. Even with the work of Darwin and Einstein in the mix, a totally unknown and invisible deity—the *logos* that was before the beginning of time (cf. John 1:1–2)—was generally incomprehensible to people, most of whom claimed educational achievements that were, in the last third of the nineteenth century, at about the eighth grade level. Fewer than ninety-five thousand youths in a national population of 76,212,168 graduated from high school in the United States in 1900, being 6.4 percent of all seventeen-year-olds.[91] At the beginning of the twentieth century about 2 percent of Americans ages 18–24 were enrolled in college or university.[92]

Jesus was a character anyone who had ever gone to a Protestant Sunday school would know or know of. Images of him appeared in church tracts, Sunday school papers and in various media of the graphic arts. Mostly the Jesuses of that era were gentle, meek and mild, entirely unthreatening, and said to be helpful. Whence that set of ideas? Mostly the work of eisegetes importing their own needs, aspirations, or ideas into their sermons, Sunday school lessons, and hymn texts. But Jesus as rescuing hero, especially appealing to sea-going mariners for whom the Hopper hymn was originally written, became a popular image of the one said, by theologians both professional and amateur, to be the Son of God.

Jesus the Lion-Heart

Not since Martin Luther's gnarly text in *Ein Feste Burg ist unser Gott* had Jesus looked so militant as he did and does in Sabine Baring-Gould's *Onward, Christian Soldiers*. Luther: "The Prince of Darkness grim, We tremble not for him; / His rage we can endure, for, lo, his doom is sure— / One little word shall fell him." And that word would come from the mouth of "The Man of God's own choosing." Baring-Gould: "Christ the royal Master / leads against the foe; / Forward into battle, / See his banners go." Here is an early form of muscular Christianity for you. No "gentle Jesus, meek and mild" about this hymn text. Real men follow Jesus, especially if he is leading an army on the way to defeat some dastardly foe. Reminiscent of the medieval crusades, he is Jesus the Lion-Heart. In times of war and general unrest, Christian poets have often reached for the more militant figures of speech to account for Jesus Christ. He may be a friend to the needy, a breast or shoulder to the troubled, a wise pilot for the captain of a foundering ship, or just the accessible surrogate for a god who must surely be in charge of this confusing world, but finally he is in the vanguard of a mighty army moving steadfastly and directly into combat with evil, assured of victory as voices of all concerned are blended together "in the triumph song." For one who would move from the resurrection narratives to the theologians' images of death and a broken Jesus locked in combat behind the tomb's heavy stone, the Baring-Gould image works. It should come as no surprise to learn that at the convention of Theodore Roosevelt's American Progressive Party (known as the Bull Moose party), he led the throng in singing Baring-Gould's hymn. The image of Jesus with jutted jaw striding into trouble as "he set his face to go to Jerusalem"[93] and directly into conflict with the powers that were would certainly have appealed to Roosevelt, the *über mensch* whose charge up San Juan Hill is the *locus classicus* of his varied public personas.

The image of Jesus the Lion-Heart has resonated well with men in the 157 years since Baring-Gould wrote the hymn. It served the Young Men's Christian Association (YMCA) well in its ministry to young males who were not embarrassed to talk about Jesus even as they lifted weights, sparred in the ring, and swam laps in the pool. Jesus had been and maybe even still was a real man, not a wimp.

In the same vein is Priscilla Owens' 1868 hymn *Jesus Saves*, in which appears such phraseology as "Onward! 'tis the Lord's command. . . . Sing in triumph o'er the tomb." This is triumphalism at its highest, evangelical triumphalism, but triumphalism none-theless. There is not a glimmer, not a suggestion of retreat. It's all out for Jesus.

Jesus as Miracle Worker

Perhaps more than any one thing, save the fact-starved proclama-tions of his resurrection, the stories of Jesus' working of so-called miracles have catapulted him into the upper regions of human imagination. "Working" is actually a key word here, since the Greek ἔργα or "works" is often used in the gospels where the word English "miracles" might be used.[94] The common defini-tion of *miracle* is "an extraordinary event manifesting divine intervention in human affairs." In the New Testament such things are called *signs and wonders* — "signs" that something big is afoot and "wonders" as in "the dumb spake, and the people wondered" (Luke 11:14b; KJV). One of the more appealing hymn texts that treats of Jesus' supposedly supernatural powers is Elvina M. Hall's *I Heard the Savior say*. It includes this remarkable and charming locution: "Lord, now indeed I find Thy power, and Thine alone / can change the leper's spots. / And melt the heart of stone." "Melt the heart of stone" suggests that Hall took meta-phorically such stories as the cleansing of the ten lepers (Matt 8:1–4, Mark 1:40–45, and Luke 5:12–16). Withal, Hall's hymn is far from the only one that celebrates Jesus as a miracle worker. That is part of the christological package connecting him with the deity from which he is said not only to have come but with which he was one and the same (John 1:1–2).

At one time or another since the Enlightenment every one of the miracle narratives in the gospels has been rationalized, some-times to death and sometimes by this author whilst homiletically engaged. Healing the blind? There are all kinds of blindness. Seeing, they do not see. Healing the deaf? Hearing, they do not hear (Matt 13:13). Yet those stories would have to be told by evan-gelists whose perceived work it was to promote Jesus as messiah. None of them could have been ignorant of the promises made on behalf of Yahweh by the First Isaiah (35:5–6): "Then shall the eyes of the blind be opened; and the ears of the dead unstopped. Then shall the lame man leap like a heart, and the tongue of the dumb shall sing."[95] Each of those, plus the lepers, finds a place in the works attributed to Jesus and celebrated in many a hymn, but nowhere more lyrically than in Hall's verse.

Jesus as Servant Missioner

The vision of Jesus as a peripatetic angel and minister of grace[96] does not emerge in biblical interpretation and theology until modern times with the advent of what has been called "the social gospel," in which Jesus is seen as the exemplar of random acts of mercy and kindness. The image is connected to some degree with Jesus as the miracle worker, though in a more credible way. That said, the Jesuses of the gospels do not necessarily come off as the Master "walking in lowly paths of service free," as Washington Gladden's hymn suggests, nor having the patience Gladden proposes as a quality. But every version of the gospel has seemed to need its own hymnody, and the beginnings of the social gospel's prominence—until the evangelical lobby tried to snuff it out with the help of the Roman Catholic hierarchy and its hatred of liberation theology—found major support in Gladden's text. So, too, Frank Mason North's *Where Cross the Crowded Ways of Life* in which Jesus is importuned to "tread the city's streets again," there to "heal these hearts of pain" as well as to assuage "woman's grief" and relieve "man's burdened toil." Though both Gladden and North wrote before the significant emergence into public life of such universal figures as Mohandas Gandhi and Mother Teresa of Calcutta, the examples of these mid-to-late twentieth-century icons fulfill the aspirations of the hymn texts of both.

Gladden and North eschewed the more graphic images of the bleeding Jesus shedding blood to pay a righteous deity for the sins of humankind as well as the crooked arm and inviting breast in and upon which wearied souls might find comfort. The emphasis in these latter-day hymns was the real world and its injustices. Into that dangerous arena Gladden and North and others who followed their lead imagined the Jesus of the gospels walking—neither striding in like Wyatt Earp to settle hash with gunslingers nor riding into town on a white horse with guns drawn, but one openly sad at "man's inhumanity to man,"[97] while, as Gladden put it, "we catch the vision" of "thy tears." The biblical connection may be to Matt 23:37, Jesus' heart-rending lament over Jerusalem in which Matthew depicts him saying that he would gather its children to him as a hen gathers her chicks. Beyond the New Testament are the Suffering Servant Songs of the Second Isaiah, especially, perhaps, the one in which the servant is depicted thus: "Surely he hath borne our griefs and carried our sorrows" (53:4–5; KJV).

The hymns of Gladden and North have served well the servant theology of Jesus and helped shape his soteriological image in service to Christianity's social mission, which may well define its relevance in this age. Homeless shelters, soup kitchens, centers for legal, medical, dental, and psychological aid have sprung up in churches not only in the cities but in suburban areas with the image of what one Detroit minister calls "Jesus the Involved."

Jesus as Countercultural Guru

Twentieth-century Christian liberalism brought forth a new hymnody that was far from the cloying piety of previous eras. S. Ralph Harlow's 1931 *O Young and Fearless Prophet* is a good example of that hymnody. Harlow saw Jesus as avatar of peacemaking and of public demonstration "against war's bloody ways" and in so doing foresaw the clergy-led demonstrations against the Vietnam War of the 1960s—such renowned figures as William Sloane Coffin and Catholic Bishop Thomas Gumbleton who made the ending of that and later wars the major motif of their public ministries. Jesus, placard in one hand, bullhorn in the other, leading a throng of demonstrators in singing, "All we are saying is give peace a chance."[98] Harlow's Jesus would have been at home in the Occupy Wall Street crowd in the autumn of 2011: "Stir up in us a protest / against our greed for wealth, / while others starve and hunger / and plead for work and health." Those words would not be popular among those parishioners who frequent St. Paul's Cathedral in London, where there was much controversy over a similar protest there in October 2011. Harlow wrote his hymn using just two theologically loaded words: *Christ's*, as in "Christ's holy sway," and *God's*, as in "God's holy way."

That portrayal of Jesus is offensive to traditional Christians, especially of the evangelical fundamentalist kind who prefer their Jesus as the sacrificial lamb for their sins and the resurrected specter up from the grave and on his way to heaven. It is likewise offensive to those who prefer the image of Jesus as personal friend and savior. The kind of picture Harlow paints of Jesus as a countercultural figure is terrifically offensive to those who cannot separate patriotism and nationalism from religion. Jesus as protest leader and peacenik does not fly in many churches.

Were more preachers to dig a little deeper in the gospels, especially Mark, they would see the kind of Jesus of whom Harlow wrote: the Jesus who said "the Sabbath was made for humankind, not humankind for the Sabbath" (Mark 2:27; NRSV)—Jesus the iconoclast whose words spoken and actions taken as depicted by the evangelist stood against the establishment's business as usual. It is such a depiction that led liberation theologians to declare that "God is on the side of the poor." Harlow's Jesus is in some ways much closer to the ones accounted for in the gospels than the Jesus of other hymnists.

Jesus as Universal Sibling

In what must have been a daring move for the time in which it was written (1908) John Oxenham's *In Christ There Is No East or West* envisioned Jesus as a universal brother to all people everywhere, at every point on the compass. It is in no way a triumphalist or aggressively missionary text. It does not call for conquering the beliefs or practices of any known faith or religion. It is a call to say goodbye to all that and serve humankind however it needs to be served by whoever can be mustered into the task. Oxenham wrote of "one great Fellowship of Love / Throughout the whole wide earth." It is well-nigh utopian, and it certainly must have seemed that and more when the hymn appeared. A far cry from the raw evangelistic fervor of Reginald Heber's *From Greenland's Icy Mountains*, the Oxenham hymn takes no account of theological differences between and among different religious expressions, saying that whoever serves the divine ends of justice and peace can and should be called God's son. There is that opening phrase "In Christ," which might give the Buddhist or Hindu pause, but if he or she reads on "Christ" will seem to be a generic term for a realized deity. "All Christly souls," Oxenham wrote, "are one in him." I think this makes no claim whatsoever that the Christian philosophical construction is to be paramount. Oxenham was writing out of his own experience as a Christian, seeming to say that what he understood of the divine initiative supposedly expressed in Jesus Christ was portable into other languages, concepts, and cultures.

It is a lovely but perhaps too optimistic, and, yes, utopian, idea about which Oxenham wrote so passionately. But, again, the hymn was written during the expansive Edwardian era and within a year after Theodore Roosevelt sent a great part of the US Navy around the world as if to flex American muscle. India still labored under the Raj, and Anglican and Methodist missionaries were still intent on christening the whole of sub-equatorial Africa. The hymn could be taken as a rebuke of all of that with its strong suggestion "Christ" meant something benignly universal into which a person of any or of no religion could find incorporation for the sake of serving human need. It is of interest that the hymn is found in several contemporary Baptist hymnals while Heber's is not.

⁓

The conclusion one can justifiably draw from the analysis is that the Jesus figure is like Gumby in that he can be twisted into just about any image a person desires. While to a liberal philosopher such as this author, the images limned by Washington Gladden, Frank Mason North, S. Ralph Harlow and John Oxenham are more appealing, the fact is that except for the gospel literature of the New Testament nothing attestable is known about the one or the ones called "Jesus." And what can be extracted from the gospel texts is sometimes contradictory, since so much of the so-called record existed in oral tradition for some indeterminate length of time. Of course, we have the written version of St. Paul's dictated epistles, or letters, all of which must date from the late forties to the late fifties CE, but outside of what appears to be a single reference to Jesus as a historical character (1 Cor 11:23–26), for Paul Jesus was the Christ, or anointed one, almost a figure of mythology. And the manner in which John begins (1:1–14), the one called "the Word" appears to be a figure of myth as well.

John's gospel sets forth the Jesus of its narrative as the *logos*, or eternal and universal creative genius. As has been observed, such a concept has all the effect of a glass of cold water thrown in the face. People of piety with needs unmet in their lives reach out not for a *logos* but for a friend, for someone who speaks their language, can appreciate their injury and deprivation. And so the poets oblige with verbal images such as the ones we have revisited in this analysis. The more fetching the image, the more it becomes a statement about a "real" Jesus. Thus, despite the toil of scholars of scripture to set the record straight, Jesus has become the friend in need and a friend indeed to those whose life circumstances demand one the likes of whom cannot be found among family, neighbors, and friends.

Is "Jesus" then that blank canvas upon which those needy paint whatever picture of him suits their needs? So it seems.

Epilogue

The communions of Christianity have tried for centuries to reach a consensus on what kind of songs and hymns work for their liturgies and other worship services. The church's expansion across cultural boundaries, thanks at first to the Constantinian embrace of the faith, complicated that effort. Christian singing surely arose out of Hebraic tradition on display in the biblical book of Psalms. The psalms are clearly poetry often ascribed to leaders (of choirs?). Some psalms have notes above them resembling in form such musical directions as *allegro moderato* or *vivace*; Psalm 7, for example, is called a *shiggaion*, which may have been a direction to sing or voice it in a meditative, somewhat emotional way. The terms *maskil* and *selah* frequently appear as notes or prompts outside the flow of verse. Psalm 4 calls for stringed instruments supposedly as accompaniment, Psalm 5 for flutes. Psalm 150 names instruments to be accompany the praise of Yahweh: trumpet, lute, harp, tambourine, pipes and cymbals.

In the Introduction we briefly traced the development of liturgical singing in the Christian tradition from chants based on biblical texts. For its musical traditions, Christianity is deeply indebted to the monastic communities in which those traditions evolved. As the Reformation encouraged the use of the vernacular in the offering of liturgy, congregational singing was made possible, first, one supposes, by the same method as in antiquity, when words and music were a matter of memory. The repertoire of congregations was greatly enhanced by the printing press and the appearance of hymnals. As literacy grew, hymns became not only a means of teaching doctrine through the singing of biblical texts and lyrics clearly taken from them, but also of community building. When early followers of Luther could and did sing, perhaps even in harmony, *Ein feste Burg ist unser Gott*, the foundations of the Roman Church could have been heard shaking.

Solid and memorable texts set to accessible and easy-to-sing melodies can be hypnotic. Think in a darker way of the German national anthem between 1933 and 1945 set to Haydn's tune Austria: *Deutschland, Deutschland über alles*. Think again of Sabine Baring-Gould's "Onward, Christian soldiers, marching as to war," sung to the martial tune by Arthur S. Sullivan. Both the German anthem and Baring-Gould's Sunday school hymn stirred souls, and still do—in the former case, with baleful effect.

As era gave way to era, Christian hymnody evolved to match the demographic, social, and theological climates. Protestant Europe of the sixteenth century onward in terms of congregational singing could be characterized as church naves full of burghers and their families filling the air with beery odors left over from Saturday night whilst pounding out C-Major hymns in 4/4 time with rhyming stanzas—each and all depicting a stern deity, battles with Satan, and admonitions to faith and hard work. English hymns—in Cromwell's time unaccompanied by the hated organ—were sparse of emotion, more Calvinist and didactic, emphasizing Sabbath obligations. As the nineteenth century dawned and England was tossed to and fro by the forces of Whigs and Tories and their counterparts in the Church of England, namely, High and Evangelical Church parties,[99] hymns took on a more pastoral tone, as in John Keble's "Blest are the pure in heart, / For they shall see our God" and Christopher Wordsworth's "Love is kind and suffers long; Love is meek and thinks no wrong; Love than death itself more strong; Therefore, give us love." Henry Alford's 1844 "Come, ye thankful people, come, / Raise the song of harvest home" became beloved in the English Church for the fall harvest festival, especially in the country parishes. One can see and hear a congregation of gentlemen farmers and their families singing it at morning service as the household servants are preparing the mid-day dinner and their counterparts of the barns and fields keep Sabbath in their own way.

And so it went on through the Industrial Revolution, through war after war. As American Christianity came into its own in a land where freedom of religion also implied freedom from religion, hymnody was adapted. We have seen how the frontier and life, for example, out on the Great Plains shaped the tenor of hymn texts. The melodic style of Stephen Foster—tunes easy to sing and hard to forget—gave such texts a memorable quality. Often enough they spoke of loss, both experienced and anticipated, of loneliness and of longing, as in "Softly and tenderly, Jesus is calling. . . . O sinner, come home."

As what are now called "mainline denominations" organized and printed their own authorized hymnals, the theological and social—and sometimes economic—characteristics of their churches were visible in the hymns admitted to their musical volumes. Larger urban and suburban churches were and are generally outfitted with quality pipe organs and choirs—or at least lead singers in them—and were, in better economic times, given stipends for their service. Thus, classical music tended to be used as voluntaries and choral pieces matched with hymns that reflected more sophisticated, sometimes even muscular but less sentimental verse and musically unhackneyed tunes and harmonies. In country churches, things were simpler. Organs, if there were any, were at first of the pump variety with their whiny sounds. Later—and not necessarily to good effect—the electronic organ made its debut. Amateur organists could not resist using the simpering tremolo effect. When organs were not available, almost every church had at least one of those upright grands.

Clergy and clergy wives of such churches often had minimal-to-adequate musical training and could drag their congregations along on simpler, well-known hymns. More ambitious leaders tried hymn-of-the-month plans to teach new tricks to old dogs. Sometimes the plans worked; sometimes they didn't. Professionally trained musicians hate to keep singing the same two dozen hymns. They hate even more so the omitting of stanzas at the direction of clock-watching clergy who want to make more time for their sermons. If there are such things as average congregations, most music in them can be graded about C-minus where quality of music chosen and performed is concerned. The argument against that kind of judgment is that a church is not a concert hall, and whatever works should be allowed to do what it does, and never mind J. S. Bach. There is even some prejudice against more classical and complicated music in such churches engendered, no doubt, by the lack of ability a) to understand it and b) to do it right, not to mention reaction to hoity-toity tastes.

Those conditions together with a dumbed-down theology were perhaps to some degree the breeding ground for what is now called "praise" music. Such music is often accompanied, led generally, by guitar, non-organ keyboard, and not infrequently percussion. The songs have umpteen verses and much refrain repetition. They appeal to television-besotted churchgoers who see and hear it at its alleged best on mega-church programs. It's smiley. It is likely to feature toe-tapping rhythm and highly personal sentiments about how much the singers love Jesus and seek to praise and please him. In the place of such presentations, one might long to hear a monastic choir chant the *Veni, creator spiritus*. A Roman Catholic who since the late 1960s has regularly attended mass at his parish church—not a cathedral or collegiate church—will seldom, if ever, have heard such a thing as the *Veni, creator*. He is more likely to have heard the "new music" that is of folk variety. That plus the vernacular of the post-Vatican II mass are said by many to have robbed the historic liturgy of its majesty and inspiration. That Catholic person's attitude toward his church and its hierarchy may well have been formed to some extent by his experience at mass. It may be no coincidence that *Humanae vitae*, promulgated a little less than three years after the implementation of the Vatican II liturgical forms, was largely ignored by American Catholics who had increasingly seen their priests leave to marry, their nuns don street clothes, and their mass turn into a hootenanny.

The Anglican maxim *Lex orandi, lex credendi* (roughly, "as we pray, so we believe") can be applied to any communion's hymnody. As we sing, so we believe. It might also be true to say "what we sing tends to shape what we believe." How might we able to tell that? Conjure up the once well-attended mainline Protestant church in the downtown of a failing city. Attend its eleven o'clock Sunday service, finding a wide choice of seats among the ocean of empty pews. The organist—still paid through a generous endowment made possible by a long-dead industrial titan who happened to have loved Bach—plays the introduction to, say, *A Mighty Fortress Is Our God.* When the first stanza begins hardly a voice is heard among the scattering of sexagenarians and septuagenarians, mostly women. It does not sound mighty. And if there is a fortress somewhere in the picture, it has been breached by an enemy. Whatever bulwark there was has failed, and there is no help at hand "amid the flood of mortal ills prevailing." The tune is familiar, the words perhaps more so. But the unmoved singers do not believe them.

Switch channels to the mega-church in a suburb of that same city, out where the oaks and maples have spread their spring branches and new leaves. The lawns are mown, the streets clear and clean, the automobiles on them new and shiny. Try if you can to find a parking spot in the vast asphalted four-acre lot. If successful, make your way into the sanctuary that reminds you, on the one hand, of a vast gymnasium, and on the other of a space-age theater. Up on the platform you see a man informally dressed, microphone attached to his headset leading ten thousand people in roaring unison through the Carl Boberg-Stuart Hine hymn *How Great Thou Art.* The musicians, who seem to come by the dozen, swell the accompaniment to double forte, the camera's eye sweeps across the rows and tiers. Women are weeping. Men are wiping their eyes. The mood is one of emotional uplift. The same can be created by a similar audience or congregation in a similar setting singing *Amazing Grace*, giving it all they've got. John Newton's conversion to evangelical Christianity was powerful and life-changing. His composition of *Amazing*

Grace was not connected with his later abolitionist views, as is commonly held—especially by those who should know better. Such hymns as *How Great Thou Art* and *Amazing Grace*, especially when sung by large numbers of people, have an almost hypnotic effect on those who sing them. I remember an occasion upon which an acquaintance of mine said, after a rendition of the Newton hymn, that, were he to hear it sung like that again, he would be forced to believe in God.

What to make of the so-called "new music" as heard, say, in a snappy-looking new parish church in a middle-class suburb? "Father Jim" is the celebrant, looking as if he were just fresh out of college, all smiles and full of bonhomie. There are two guitars, a set of hand bells, a keyboard and a drum set to back up the singing, which seems to defy the need for a dependable rhythm. But off they go, first announcing, "Our opening song is #383 in the book," and then begins the strumming, the beat, and the bells. The lyrics sometimes rhyme, some times not. They are vaguely related to scripture texts or images, often highly personal with first-person pronouns here and there, such as *Jesu, Jesu, Fill Us with Your Love*. The congregation seems oddly unengaged, content to watch the musicians enjoy themselves in their performance. Some people sing along, others tap their feet, yet others stare straight ahead. The best sung of any part of the mass is the "Alleluia" before and after the gospel reading. It is often accompanied by brass instruments, especially on major feast days. Withal, it is difficult to tell how much the hymns and songs have been affected by belief, and how much they are an effect of belief.

In a Catholic parish in a similar demographic setting one can hear several of the old Protestant stand-bys: *Praise to the Lord, the Almighty, the King of Creation, When morning Gilds the Skies* and *Lo, He Comes with Clouds, Descending*. At a recent Christmas Eve mass my wife and I attended, the four Christmas carols used were Protestant in origin, save *Stille Nacht*. In the former category, it seems that the metric nature of the score, well matched with the text, pretty well carries the congregation along; in the latter, the sheer familiarity with the seasonal words and music creates, wherever they are said and sung, a community of believers at least in the moment.

In a small, rural church, the minister arrives at the last minute, having just finished an earlier service for another congregation on his circuit. She or he hurriedly consults with the pianist about what hymns will be sung, and shortly the service begins. Today there are fewer than twenty people in the pews. They are bidden to stand and sing a certain hymn. They try to follow the pianist, who plays by ear, and either too loudly or too softly, too fast or too slow. They sing all five stanzas of the chosen hymn and appear thankful to take their seats and listen to the minister lead the responsive reading, read the Bible lessons and preach the sermon. The singing for the congregation has been a trial, even as the accompaniment was more than the pianist could really manage. Nothing particularly edifying had occurred in the music department, and the chorus of *Bringing in the Sheaves* will lurch through the congregation's collective minds for the next day or so.

Whatever the hymns, however accompanied and sung by whatever the congregation, the central connective tissue seems to be the image of Jesus. Not only theologically is he said to be the divine power (*logos*) become flesh, but in a practical way that seems to be "true" as well. In many of the hymn texts quoted from and analyzed in this book, praises and pleadings alike are made to "the Lord," who sometimes appears to be the transcendent one (the unseen God), other times the immanent one (the physical Jesus who lived in such and such a time and place, was born of a woman and lived among the people of his day as one of them).[100] In any event, Jesus emerges from much hymn singing as something like the "friend" of Joseph Scriven's 1855 text—a highly personal earth-bound divinity, almost as accessible as the person in the next room or just down the street, as someone who knows of an individual's trials and tribulations and can and will relieve the petitioner of their onerous burden.

Not much room is allowed for that Jesus in systematic theology and creedal statements. It is highly doubtful that Scriven was thinking of the Second Person of the Trinity when he wrote *What a Friend We Have in Jesus.* It is likewise doubtful that he had the Pauline Christ in mind as portrayed as willing victim (Phil 2:8), "the first born of all creation" (Col 1:15), or yet the raised or unraised Christ of Paul's argument in 1 Corinthians 15. Quite different in tone than, for example, the hymn for Ascensiontide—*Crown Him with Many Crowns*—the Scriven text appears to represent where millions of Christians in the Western world—especially Protestants—are with respect to their religion. They embrace "Jesus" as an animist grasps an amulet. They breathe his name in times of stress and trouble. They imagine his presence around them, knowing quite well what he looks like, thanks to artists over time who have painted Jesus, sculpted him, and otherwise graphically represented them according to their own private vision, such as Sallman's slightly simpering, tanned Anglo with long, flowing hair that glows as if a stylist had applied a rinse.

To Sallman's credit, the face is kindly, open, and unthreatening. There is no obvious judgment in the clear-eyed look of his Jesus. To men inwardly troubled by the slightest effeminacy in a man, Sallman's *Head of Christ* might be a bit off-putting. But when push comes to shove, a kindly face saying that it is Jesus will probably suffice. And that seems to be the Jesus to whom generations of Christians have sung, of whom they have made a friend—one they could count on because he never was perceived as turning his back—or his face—away. Theologians alternately scratch their heads and beat them against a wall because they cannot get their catechetic Jesus firmly in place with the masses. But just as with so many of those nineteenth- and twentieth-century hymn writers, the theology and piety of the "friend Jesus" has carried the day.

This image, and a considerable portion of the hymnody of Protestantism, owes its power to need-based human imagination bolstered by sentiment. In these pages we have treated of such popular hymns as *Softly and Tenderly, Jesus Is Calling.* The most likely biblical allusions to such an idea are found in the 23rd Psalm that depicts Yahweh as an attentive shepherd, in Isa 40:11

("He shall feed his flock like a shepherd; he will gather the lambs in his arms and carry them in his bosom and gently lead those that are with young"), and in these words credited to Jesus by Matt at 11:28: "Come to me all ye that labor and are heavy-laden, and I will give you rest." Undeniably, such language portrays a deity that all but those with the hardest of hearts would reject. To human beings of all sorts and conditions such images proffer comfort and emotional sustenance in critical times of confusion and helplessness. It is precisely then that those who have some-how in some time and in some place been nurtured, however su-perficially, in Sunday school Christianity reach back into memory for the friend they once had in Jesus and with whom hope to reconnect. It is the thesis of this book that those circumstances have made hymns like *Softly and Tenderly* perennial favorites of typical Protestant Christians—and even occasionally Catholic Christians—never minding the sophisticated theological systems being erected and ever shifting philosophical tides and currents.

If that thesis is valid, comes next the question of what exactly religion is. Is it psychiatric therapy on the cheap? Is it an emo-tional teddy bear? Is it really ever so private a thing as all that? In my 2012 book *Long Live Salvation by Works: A Humanist Manifesto*, a case is made that a religion that matters engages its adherents in the here-and-now of life, provides a focus on the biosphere start-ing with human beings individually and collectively, rejects ex-planations of things that fail to appeal to observation and reason and, finally, advocates ways to live sustainably and in harmony with the rest of life: animal, vegetable and mineral. Such hymns as Clifford Bax's 1919 text, *Turn Back, O Man*, a direct reaction to the Great War, get at that understanding of religion, as does Harry Emerson Fosdick's *God of Grace, and God of Glory*, albeit with a firm theism at the root of the latter. Samuel Longfellow's *God of the Earth, the Sky, the Sea!* and Folliott Pierpont's *For the Beauty of the Earth*, both published in 1864, echo the motif of the much better known 1712 text by Joseph Addison *The Spacious Firmament on High*, which celebrates nature in elevated and el-evating prose that calls those who sing them to celebrate and care for Earth and all who dwell therein.

If Christianity, especially its Protestant branch, is to attain the kind of relevance to life outside of its piety, and if it continues to use hymnody as a bonding agent, a new set of texts along the lines of Bax's, Fosdick's, Pierpont's and Addison's will be necessary. I have thought for a long time that the verse of such twentieth-century poets as the late Gary J. Frahm, an Episcopal priest who served congregations in Iowa from 1963–83 might be set to singable tunes. What believer will adapt Frahm's poem "To Jesus on the Rood, XIV" and set it to music? I would love to hear how some adapter would voice Frahm's lines, *I sometimes think I have, great Son of God / an ever so feeble grasp of who you are. / Yet, knowing but ill one tiny piece of sod, / how shall I think to comprehend a star?*[101]

Notes

1. G. Abbott-Smith, *A Manual Greek Lexicon*, 455.

2. G. Autenrieth, *Homeric Dictionary*, 276.

3. Ignatius, *To the Ephesians*, in C. Richardson, 89.

4. J. Marquand, *B. F.'s Daughter*, 322.

5. *The Pilgrim Hymnal, The Hymnal 1982*, and *Rejoice: The Free-Will Baptist Hymnal*.

6. G. K. Chesterton, *O God of Earth and Altar*, found in the hymnals discussed in text above.

7. Journal of the Proceedings of the General Convention of the Protestant Episcopal Church.

8. H. W. Longfellow, "Paul Revere's Ride," 276.

9. Wesley wrote of that experience: "About a quarter before nine, while he was describing the change which God works in the heart through faith in Christ, I felt my heart strangely warmed. I felt I did trust in Christ, Christ alone, for salvation; and an assurance was given me that He had taken away my sins, even mine, and saved me from the law of sin and death." (in A. Outler, *John Wesley*, 66)

10. Hymn by W. Thompson, *Softly and Tenderly Jesus Is Calling*.

11. *The English Hymnal*, 591.

12. T. Wolfe, *The Hills Beyond*, 106–7.

13. Jefferson's Letter to the Baptist Association of Danbury Connecticut, Jan. 1, 1802.

14. R. Balmer, *The Making of Evangelicalism*, 9.

15. A. Porterfield, *Conceived in Doubt*, 78–112.

16. E. Pagels, *Beyond Belief*, 50–73.

17. J. M. K. London, *Bright Talks on Favourite Hymns*, 79.

18. "When lilacs last in the dooryard bloom'd, /And the great star early drooped in the western sky in the night, I mourn'd, and yet shall mourn with ever-returning spring."

19. R. Morgan, *Then Sings My Soul*, Bk. 1, 271.

20. *The Princeton Seminary Bulletin*, 210–16.

21. R. Morgan, *Then Sings My Soul*, Bk. 1, 271.

22. H. Rodeheaver, *Triumphant Service Songs*, #189.

23. T. Brown and H. Butterworth, *The Story of the Hymns and Tunes*, 165.

24. R. Morgan, *Then Sings My Soul*, Bk. 2, 145.

25. Docetism was an early "heresy" advocated by those who insisted that Jesus had only seemed human—from the Greek verb , to "seem" or "suppose."

26. H. Rodeheaver, *Triumphant Service Songs*, #229.

27. E. MacHugh, *Treasury of Gospel Hymns and Poems*, #122.

28. A. Bailey, *The Gospel in Hymns*, 405. W. Reynolds, *Hymns of Our Faith*, 401.

29. A. Bailey, *The Gospel in Hymns*, 507. W. Reynolds, *Hymns of Our Faith*, 387.

30. H. Rodeheaver, *Triumphant Service Songs*, #206.

31. A. Bailey, *The Gospel in Hymns*, 503. R. Morgan, *Then Sings My Soul*, Bk. 1, 179. W. Reynolds, *Hymns of Our Faith*, 312.

32. R. Morgan, *Then Sings My Soul*, Bk. 2, 183. W. Reynolds, *Hymns of Our Faith*, 421.

33. A. Bailey, *The Gospel in Hymns*, 503.

34. T. Brown and H. Butterworth, *The Story of the Hymns and Tunes*, 374. W. Reynolds, *Hymns of Our Faith*, 320.

35. T. Brown and H. Butterworth, *The Story of the Hymns and Tunes*, 26.

36. *The Pilgrim Hymnal*, #284.

37. *The United Methodist Hymnal*, #509.

38. *Rejoice: The Free Will Baptist Hymnal*, #605.

39. R. Morgan, *Then Sings My Soul*, Bk. 1, 177. W. Reynolds, *Hymns of Our Faith*, 254.

40. F. Dyer, *A Compendium of the War of Rebellion*.

41. R. Morgan, *Then Sings My Soul*, Bk. 2, 125. W. Reynolds, *Hymns of Our Faith*, 249.

42. R. Morgan, *Then Sings My Soul*, Bk. 2, 189. W. Reynolds, *Hymns of Our Faith*, 377.

43. R. Morgan, *Then Sings My Soul*, Bk. 1, 139. W. Reynolds, *Hymns of Our Faith*, 431.

44. R. Morgan, *Then Sings My Soul*, Bk. 2, 239. W. Reynolds, *Hymns of Our Faith*, 365.

45. R. Balmer, *The Making of Evangelicalism*, 20, 21.

46. The Methodist version of canon law, its guide to policy and procedure.

47. W. Hudson, *Religion in America*, 342–44.

48. A. Bailey, *The Gospel in Hymns*, 370. W. Reynolds, *Hymns of Our Faith*, 244.

49. A. Bailey, *The Gospel in Hymns*, 372.

50. *The Pilgrim Hymnal*, 399. *The Hymnal of the Protestant Episcopal Church, USA* (1940), 557. *Rejoice: The Free Will Baptist Hymn Book*, 614.

51. S. Calthrope, *The Realities of War in Crimea*, 132.

52. W. Walker, *A History of the Christian Church*, 101.

53. A. Tennyson, *Complete Poems*, 430, 432.

54. K. Osbeck, *101 More Hymn Stories*, 237.

55. W. Reynolds, *Hymns of Our Faith*, 384. R. Morgan, *Then Sings My Soul*, Bk. 1, 263.

56. Sources vary on these details, whether the engagements were in New Jersey or Pennsylvania.

57. W. Reynolds, *Hymns of Our Faith*, 316.

58. W. Reynolds, *Hymns of Our Faith*, 306.

59. Second and third stanzas with direct references to Jesus Christ were appended to this text by Charles E. Prior (1856–1927), a banker by trade and a musician by choice. Born in Bridgeport, Connecticut, he lived in Jewett City for many years, where he was active in musical leadership for Congregational and Baptist Churches.

60. W. Reynolds, *Hymns of Our Faith*, 260.

61. D. Faust, *This Republic of Suffering*, 266–67.

62. W. Reynolds, *Hymns of Our Faith*, 403.

63. *Jesus, I My Cross Have Taken*, St. 4, in *The Pilgrim Hymnal*, 429.

64. W. Reynolds, *Hymns of Our Faith*, 249. Archives of the Old Rugged Cross Historical Museum, Reed City, MI.

65. See Exod 20:4, Deut 5:8.

66. A possible allusion to Ps 49:7, which suggests that the shields of a conquered army as trophies of victory belong to Yahweh, to whom the psalm gives credit for victory, Yahweh being *a great King over all the earth.*

67. E. L. Doctorow, *The March.*

68. D. Chapman, *Ancient Jewish and Christian Perceptions of Crucifixion*, 86–89.

69. W. Reynolds, *Hymns of Our Faith*, 301.

70. W. Hudson, *Religion in America*, 311.

71. W. Reynolds, *Hymns of Our Faith*, 375.

72. W. Reynolds, *Hymns of Our Faith*, 216, based on a 1917 letter for E. H. Greeley, a missionary who worked with Stead.

73. W. Reynolds, *Hymns of Our Faith*, 396.

74. W. Reynolds, *Songs of Glory*, 126.

75. S. Harlow, *A Life after Death.*

76. "When the days drew near for him [Jesus] to be taken up, he set his face to go to Jerusalem" (NSRV). The translation of "set his face" might better be rendered as "he stiffened his face," as in jaw jutted out in determination.

77. C. Dickens, *A Christmas Carol*, 14.

78. *The Book of Common Prayer*, 225.

79. A. Bailey, *The Gospel in Hymns*, 471–72. W. Reynolds, *Hymns of Our Faith*, 378.

80. H. Fosdick, *The Manhood of the Master*.

81. H. Fosdick, *The Living of These Days*, 193–94.

82. R. Heber, *From Greenland's Icy Mountains* (1819), St. 1.

83. H. Fosdick, *Living of These Days*, 207.

84. W. H. Parker (1885): "Tell me the stories of Jesus I love to hear; / Things I would ask Him to tell me if He were here: / Scenes by the way-side, tales of the sea, / Stories of Jesus, Tell them to me. // First let me hear how the children Stood round His knee, / I shall imagine His blessings rest on me; / Words full of kindness, Deeds full of grace, / All in the brightness Of Jesus' face" (St. 1 and 2).

85. T. M. Luhrmann, *When God Talks Back*, 74.

86. Linus Van Pelt, brother of Lucy Van Pelt, is a character in the on-going comic strip *Charlie Brown*, created by the late Charles M. Schulz. Linus is depicted as carrying his security blanket everywhere.

87. J. Kugel, *How to Read the Bible*, 131.

88. Smith. *The Sacrificial Rituals*.

89. Peter Scholtes and Carolyn Arends.

90. W. Reynolds, *Hymns of Our Faith*, 384.

91. US Bureau of the Census.

92. US Department of Education.

93. Luke 9:51b (NRSV): The Greek at that place is literally "stiffened his face," as in a set jaw and fearless eye.

94. *Interpreter's Dictionary of the Bible*, Vol. K–Q, 394.

95. G. F. Handel's rendition of the text for the recitative for counter-tenor, Part I of "Messiah."

96. An allusion to Shakespeare's line from Hamlet, act I, scene iv, l. 38.

97. R. Burns, "Man was Made to Mourn."

98. A 1969 lyric by Yoko Ono.

99. See Anthony Trollope's *Barchester Towers* for pointed illustrations of this phenomenon.

100. Such a statement—as in one of the Great Thanksgiving prayers of the Episcopal Church's 1979 *Book of Common Prayer*, e.g. "he lived as one of us, yet without sin" (p. 374)—is in need of rational correction.

101. G. J. Frahm, *Summer's Lease*, 87.

_____ _anual Greek Lexicon of the New Testament. _____ &T Clark, 1956.

_____ . Homeric Dictionary for Schools and Colleges. _____ American Book Company, 1876.

_____ _panion to the Song Book of the Salvation Army. _____ alvationist Publishing and Supplies Ltd., 1961.

_____ ard. The Gospel in Hymns. New York, NY: _____ ner's Sons, 1950.

Balmer, Randall. *The Making of Evangelicalism: From Revivalism to Politics and Beyond.* Waco, TX: Baylor University Press, 2010.

Barrows, Cliff and Donald P. Hustad. *Crusaders Hymns.* Carol Stream, IL: Hope Publishing Co., 1966.

Barr, Robert. *Praise Ye the Lord!* Toronto, ONT, CA: Evangelical Publishers, 1949.

Bell, George A. and Hubert P. Main, ed. *Hymns of Praise with Tunes.* Chicago: Bigelow & Main, 1884.

Blanchard, Kathleen. *Stories of Favorite Hymns.* Grand Rapids, MI: Zondervan Publishing House, 1949.

Book of Common Prayer, The. New York, NY: Oxford University Press, 1928

Brown, Theron and Hezekiah Butterworth. *The Story of the Hymns and Tunes.* New York, NY: American Tract Society, 1906.

Burrage, Henry S. *Baptist Hymn Writers and Their Hymns.* Portland, ME: Brown, Thurston & Co., 1888.

Calthorpe, Somerset J. G. *The Realities of War in the Crimea, by an Officer on the Staff.* London, G.B.: John Murray, 1857.

Cameron, Ron, ed. *The Other Gospels.* Philadelphia: The Westminster Press, 1982.

Chapman, David W. *Ancient Jewish and Christian Perceptions of Crucifixion.* Grand Rapids, MI: Baker Academic, 2010.

Commager, Henry Steele. *The American Mind.* New Haven, CT: Yale University Press, 1950.

Cook, Harry T. *Long Live Salvation by Works: A Humanist Manifesto.* Salem, OR: Polebridge Press, 2012.

Dickens, Charles. *A Christmas Carol.* London, GB: Chapman & Hall, 1843.

Doctorow, E. L. *The March.* New York, NY: Random House, 2005.

Dyer, Frederick H. *A Compendium of the War of Rebellion.* New York, NY: Thomas Yoseloff Publisher, 1959.

Emurian, Ernest K. *Living Stories of Famous Hymns.* Boston, MA: W.A. Wilder, 1955.

The English Hymnal. London, GB: Oxford University Press, 1906

Faust, Drew Gilpin. *This Republic of Suffering: Death and the American Civil War.* New York, NY: Alfred A. Knopf, 2008.

Fosdick, Harry Emerson. *The Living of These Days.* New York, NY: Harper & Brothers, 1956.

Fosdick, Harry Emerson. *The Manhood of the Master.* New York, NY: Grosset & Dunlap, 1913.

Frahm, G.J. *Summer's Lease.* Sioux Center, IA. Dordt College Press, 1989

Frykholm, Amy Johnson. *Rapture Culture: Let Behind in Evangelical America.* New York, NY: Oxford University Press, 1999.

Harlow, S. Ralph. *A Life after Death.* New York, NY: Doubleday & Co, 1961.

Hooper, William Lloyd. *Church Music in Transition.* Nashville, TN: Broadman Press, 1963.

Hudson, Winthrop S. *Religion in America.* New York: Charles Scribner's Sons, 1965.

The Hymnal 1982. New York, NY: The Church Hymnal Corporation, 1986.

The Interpreter's Dictionary of the Bible. Vol. K–Q. New York: NY, Abington Press, 1962.

Kugel, James. *How to Read the Bible.* New York, NY: Free Press, 2008.

Larson, Edward J. *Summer of the Gods: The Scopes Trial and American's Continuing Debate Over Science and Religion.* New York, NY: Basic Books,1997

London, J. M. K. *Bright Talks on Favourite Hymns.* Chicago, IL: The Religious Tract Society; John C. Winston Co., ca. 1916

Longfellow, Henry Wadsworth. "The Landlord's Tale: Paul Revere's Ride." *Tales of a Wayside Inn: Poems of Longfellow.* New York, NY. The Modern Library, 1956.

Lurhmann, T. M. *When God Talks Back: Understanding the American Evangelical Relationship with God.* New York, NY: Knopf, 2012.

MacHugh, Edward, ed. *The Treasury of Gospel Hymns and Poems.* Chicago, IL. The Rodeheaver, Hall-Mack Company, 1938

Mack, Burton L. *The Lost Gospel: The Book of Q & Christian Origin.* New York, NY: HarperSanFrancisco, 1993.

Marquand, John P. *B. F.'s Daughter.* New York, Boston, MA: Little, Brown and Company, 1946.

Marty, Martin E., and R. Scott Appleby, ed. *Fundamentalisms Observed.* Chicago: University of Chicago Press, 1991.

Meeks, Wayne A. *The First Urban Christians: The Social World of the Apostle Paul.* New Haven, CT: Yale University Press, 1983.

Morgan, Robert J. *Then Sings My Soul: 150 of the World's Greatest Hymn Stories.* Book 1. Nashville, TN: Thomas Nelson, 2003.

———. *Then Sings My Soul: 150 of the World's Greatest Hymn Stories.* Book 2. Nashville, TN: Thomas Nelson, 2004.

The New Oxford Annotated Bible with the Apocrypha: Revised Standard Version. New York, NY: Oxford University Press, 1991

Ninde, Edward S. *The Story of the American Hymn.* New York, NY: Abingdon Press, 1921.

Osbeck, Kenneth W. *101 More Hymn Stories.* Grand Rapids, MI: Kregel Publications, 1985.

———. *Amazing Grace.* Grand Rapids, MI: Kregel Publications, 1990.

Outler, Albert C., ed. *John Wesley.* New York, NY: Oxford University Press, 1964.

Page, Christopher. *The Christian West and Its Singers: The First Thousand Years*. New Haven, CT: Yale University Press, 2011.

Pagels, Elaine. *Beyond Belief: The Secret Gospel of Thomas*. New York, NY: Random House, 2003.

The Pilgrim Hymnal. Rev. ed. Boston, MA: The Pilgrim Press, 1935.

Porterfield, Amanda. *Conceived in Doubt: Religion and Politics in the New American Nation*. Chicago, IL: University of Chicago Press, 2012.

Princeton Theological Bulletin. Vol. 28, 2 (2007).

Rable, George C. *God's Almost Chosen People: A Religious History of the American Civil War*. Chapel Hill, NC: The University of North Carolina Press, 2010.

Raser, Harold E. *Phoebe Palmer, Her Life and Thought*. Lewiston, NY: Edwin Mellen Press, 1987.

Rejoice: The Free Will Baptist Hymn Book. Nashville, TN: The National Association of Free Will Baptists, Inc., 1988.

Reynolds, William J. *Hymns of Our Faith*. Nashville, TN: Broadman Press, 1964.

———. *Songs of Glory*. Grand Rapids, MI: Baker Publishing Group, 1996.

Richardson, Cyril C., ed. *Early Christian Fathers*. Vol.1. Philadelphia, PA. The Westminster Press, 1953.

Rodeheaver, Homer A., ed. *Triumphant Service Songs*. Winona Lake, MN: Rodeheaver-Mack, 1934.

Smith, Mark S. *The Sacrificial Rituals and Myths of the Goodly Gods, KTU/CAT 1.23: Royal Constructions of Opposition, Intersection, Integration and Domination* (Society of Biblical Literature/Brill, 2006)

Smith, Oswald. *Oswald Smith's Hymn Stories*. Winona Lake, MN: The Rodeheaver Co., 1963.

Taves, Ann. *Fits, Trances & Visions: Experiencing Religion and Explaining Experience from Wesley to James*. Princeton, NJ: Princeton University Press, 1999.

Tennyson, Lord Alfred. *The Complete Poems of Tennyson*. New York, NY: The Modern Library, 1938.

Trollope, Anthony. *Barchester Towers*. New York, NY: Penguin Books, 2003.

Walker, Williston. *A History of the Christian Church,* rev. ed. New York, NY: Charles Scribner's Sons, 1959.

Whiston, William, trans. *The Works of Josephus Complete and Unabridged.* Peabody, MA: Hendrickson Publishers, 1987.

Wolfe, Thomas. *The Hills Beyond.* New York, NY: Harper & Brothers, 1935.

Other hymn collections consulted include: *American Baptist Hymnal, Baptist Hymnal, The Lutheran Hymnal* (1941), *The United Methodist Hymnal* (1989), and *Presbyterian Hymnal* (1990).

Index

About the Author

Harry T. Cook is a graduate of Albion College, Albion, Michigan, and of Garrett-Evangelical Theological Seminary at Northwestern University with honors in Hebrew. He is the author of several books, including *Long Live Salvation by Works* (2012), *Resonance: Biblical Texts Speaking to 21st Century Inquirers* (2011), *Christianity Beyond Creeds* (1997), *Sermons of a Devoted Heretic* (1999), *Seven Sayings of Jesus* (2001), *Findings: Exegetical Essays on the Gospel*

Lections (2003) and *Asking: Inquirers in Conversation* (2010). He also wrote a biographical essay for *Life of Courage: Sherwin Wine and Humanistic Judaism* (2003). Recently retired after 42 years of active ministry in the Episcopal Church, he covered religion and wrote a weekly column on ethics and public policy for the Detroit Free Press in the 1980s and '90s.

CPSIA information can be obtained at www.ICGtesting.com
Printed in the USA
BVOW020444170613

323406BV00007B/19/P